EX AND THE CITY

Alexandra Heminsley is a freelance journalist and broadcaster. She is a contributing editor for *Elle* magazine, and writes regularly for the *Telegraph*, *Observer*, *londonpaper* and *Time Out* as well as reviewing on BBC Radio 2's arts show *The Weekender* and appearing as a panelist on the Simon Mayo Book Club on BBC Radio Five Live.

EX AND THE CITY

YOU'RE NOBODY 'TIL SOMEBODY DUMPS YOU

ALEXANDRA HEMINSLEY

PAN BOOKS

First published 2007 by Pan Books
an imprint of Pan Macmillan Ltd
Pan Macmillan, 20 New Wharf Road, London N1 9RR
Basingstoke and Oxford
Associated companies throughout the world
www.panmacmillan.com

ISBN 978-0-330-45242-7

1 3 5 7 9 8 6 4 2

A CIP catalogue record for this book is available
from the British Library.

Typeset by SetSystems Ltd, Saffron Walden, Essex
Printed and bound in Great Britain by
Mackays of Chatham plc, Chatham, Kent

Visit **www.panmacmillan.com** to read more about all our books
and to buy them. You will also find features, author interviews and
news of any author events, and you can sign up for e-newsletters
so that you're always first to hear about our new releases.

Contents

Introduction, 1

1 Getting Dumped, 9

2 You're Nobody 'Til Somebody Dumps You:
The Heartbroken in History, 29

3 The First Twenty-Four Hours, 59

4 The First Twenty-Four Hours (of War):
Lily's Battle Tactics, 81

5 The Rebound, 97

6 Drunk on Love: The Science of Heartache, 127

7 The Hermit Phase, 143

8 I Will Survive: The Healing Power of Music, 163

9 Dumping DNA, 191

10 We Need to Talk: What He Says vs What He Means, 215

11 Dumped from Celebville, 235

12 The Departure Lounge, 265

13 The Happy Ending, 271

Acknowledgements, 287

For all the boys who swept me off my feet
– then left me there.
And for all the girls who picked me up again.

I told you I'd be fine.

On winning her Best Actress Oscar for *Walk the Line*, **Reese Witherspoon** dedicated her award to an unlikely bunch of guys, confessing:

'Every time I got dumped, I always fantasized that one day the guy would be sorry – and I would go on stage and tell him what I thought. So, for all the boys who ever dumped me, this is for you.'

For this, I will always love her, particularly as she was going through a divorce a year later. You see, it happens to the best of us.

Introduction

I was born on Valentine's Day. My parents, a 22-year-old British Army officer and a love-struck flamenco dancer from the West Indies, foresaw a life of romantic happiness for their first-born. My heart-shaped face, my saintly middle name (Valentine), and my apposite birth date could only lead to passion and romance wherever I deigned to tread.

Instead, I just kept getting dumped. Dumped in a restaurant, dumped in a stairwell, dumped in a graveyard – it never seemed to matter. Wherever I deigned to tread, I was trod on. If Dumped were a place, the mayor would have given me the keys to the city by now. Indeed, if Dumped were a kingdom, I would be its queen.

There's always a moment when you've just been freshly dumped. Maybe you know the one: you're at a party, or in a bar, feeling like you've recently been flayed. It's exactly as if you've got no skin on – just a cocktail dress straight on top of organs. You're standing around, painfully aware of the nothingness at your side where your boyfriend often used to stand. You see a woman approaching from the other side of the room. It's always the same kind of person: maybe they mean well, but they're essentially nosy. And bossy. The sort who can say 'You look great!' and make it sound like an accusation.

Anyway, she crosses the room, spots the red around the rims of your eyes, and edges in for the kill. She's quivering with enthusiasm, her head tilted in that aggressively caring manner. 'Hi there, how *are* you?'

You rub your lips together against your teeth, stoically jutting your chin out a little. 'Oh, fine, fine. You know how it is.'

'I was so sorry to hear about you and x.'

'Yes, well, you know how it is.'

You know it's coming. There is never a break-up without this moment. *Don'taskmedon'taskmedon'taskme.*

'So . . . was it your decision or his?'

Sheaskedmesheaskedmesheaskedme. Bitch. 'Well, um, actually, it was his. You know how it is.'

There it is: number one of the many horrors in any break-up. Heartache and loss can be excruciatingly painful and cripplingly sad – whoever's decision it was to end the relationship, and whatever the reasons were. But the sting of being dumped is a unique pain. Having to admit that your heart has been ripped in two by a guy who's decided he's no longer interested in you is almost as painful as being dumped itself.

But why? What the hell is it that's inflicting this perceived humiliation? A break-up is rarely one person's fault more than the other. And even if it was, can you seriously name a dumpee who has emerged from the experience anything other than happier than she was beforehand? Of course not. The unique nature of any dumpee's agony means that you will almost always resurface wiser and have more fun. Meanwhile, the dumper often scarpers, jumping from one relationship to another, desperately trying to avoid getting 'found out' for not being perfect. Tsk.

Don't get me wrong – I am not suggesting that Dumped is a happy kingdom, littered as it is with photographs hastily torn in two, beheaded flowers and sweatshirts that 'just smell of him'. Its inhabitants are usually shoddily dressed in odd socks, lying prone on sofas with melted pots of ice cream dangling from one hand and a box of tissues from the other. Sometimes, in a leafy glade next to the stream there are some tables and disco balls. Upon those tables are girls gripping alcopops, dancing frenziedly to 'I Will Survive' – arms aloft, feet tapping, eyes glistening. But the teary streaks of mascara are giving them away. They're not enjoying their stay in Dumped any more than the workaholics sitting on the grassy verge, whose rictus grins, immaculately pressed workwear and unnatural commitment to the office are giving them away.

You see, no one *wants* to be there, but most of the time it's the only way to get somewhere better. Think of it as a busy airport when your flight's delayed on the way to a fabulous, much longed-for holiday. You genuinely believe you are trapped in that hell for ever. But you will take off eventually, and then . . . sunshine!

Visitors to the kingdom of Dumped usually try to leave as fast as they can, and fair enough. But one thing's for sure – *never* believe a girl who says that she hasn't been there. She's either lying, or suffering from a serious case of misguided pride. Because it's happened more than once to pretty much everyone. And it hurts just as much every time whether they were thirteen or one hundred and thirteen. Believe me.

I got sick of hiding it. Yes, I was prepared to see things through. Yes, I was prepared to take emotional risks and give things another chance. Yes, I was prepared to say how I felt first, even if it meant he might not reciprocate. And yes, it got me dumped. So I thought: know your enemy. What is it about getting dumped that makes it such a unique agony? How can I find out everything that there is to know about it, and get over it? So I did. And by the time I had, I saw getting dumped as a badge of honour, not a source of shame. And so should you. Trust me, I'm the Queen of Dumped.

1

Getting Dumped

Until I went for a pizza after work a few years ago I had filed getting dumped under 'inconveniently upsetting' rather than 'heartbreaking'. I'd never been dumped from a grown-up relationship, and to be honest, I wasn't that sure what all the fuss was about. Of course, it would be annoying, or a dent to anyone's pride, but surely not deserving of the wailing it induced in the girls I'd known in my teens or early twenties. Why on earth did people need to take days off work? Or talk about it all the time?

How quickly we forget. How quickly we are reminded.

Oh, I knew there was a bit of a storm brewing that night. Not even an actual storm, more like the emotional equivalent of that very gusty, slightly creepy hint-of-rain

11

kind of weather – the sort that blows a lot of dust and random three-day-old newspaper pages up into your face. (And sometimes, usually when you're feeling particularly wretched, a cigarette butt.) But I didn't think it was going to be Armageddon, I didn't even think it was going to be close. I was a little nervous, but deep down I was feeling pretty confident. In fact, I was even feeling a little empowered – a feisty woman of the new millennium. All we needed to do was to get a few things straight about the way he'd been treating me, which would be easily sorted out, and then it would be plain sailing. I had a clear mental image of myself expressing my frustrations and anxieties in a level-headed, firm but courteous manner. I wouldn't point my finger, but from time to time I would make firm eye contact with my head tilted to one side, artfully using my well-honed communication skills to convey that while I understood him, I wasn't to be messed with. Perhaps the woman at the table next to me would assume I was a hotshot lawyer, able to turn any situation to my advantage. And the waiters would lean languorously against the bar discussing how lucky Nate was to have a girl like me. So beautiful, but so strong. And yet so understanding.

I had pretty much worked out what I was or wasn't going to compromise on, and while I wasn't looking forward to the conversation, I was looking forward to it being over. It was all going to go my way. I had the skills and the spirit. All I had to do was use them.

Nate and I got to the restaurant and I took a surreptitious look around. This would do. An elegant pizza place, classy but not overwhelming. Smart enough for neither of us to make a scene, but not so chichi as to be intimidating in case I needed to take my gesticulation skills up a notch. This was definitely the kind of place sophisticated lawyers came to grab a quick bite before nipping off to the Curzon to see an enlightening yet life-affirming Iranian short film. I was still in control.

I can't stress enough how regularly I was in control of things. It's just that quite often it was only for short, fifteen-minute bursts. Again, I can't emphasize enough how awe-inspiring these short bursts must have been to those younger and less worldly wise than myself, or even to whose who weren't. But, from time to time, I did wish that these surges of empowerment went on for longer. I was actually quite looking forward to giving my over-developed communications skills a bit of an airing; to laying out my well prepared, reasoned and firm but fair arguments. But we had barely ordered when I was informed that it was all over.

'What, you and me? Completely over? With no discussion, no trying to make it work? Even after a couple of years of really great stuff?' I tried to do a huffy, disdainful exhalation of air from my bottom lip, but a tiny – seriously tiny, smaller than a grain of rice really – piece of breadstick became caught in the crossfire, landing like a grenade on the end of a prong of his fork. He didn't mention it, or condescend to brush it away. He just looked at it in an understanding way, as if he were imagining how difficult it must be to be me.

'Yes, I can't keep this up any more,' he replied, with a side helping of immense and earnest patience. His tone was now that of a teacher who'd had a long day, and was looking forward to a warm, relaxing bath – but who wasn't going to give up on that really dumb kid at the back of the class first.

'Keep this up? I didn't realize it was an endurance test. No one was forcing you to go out with me, were they? And what about New York? You've been promising to go with me for over a year – were you lying all that time?'

'No, of course not. Don't be silly. I'd love to take you, but I just can't.'

'Don't be silly?! I love you, I thought you loved me, and I have been having rather a nice time being your girlfriend – have you just been going along with this under sufferance?'

'Well, I haven't been enjoying myself for several months.'

One should never underestimate the power of the passive-aggressive statement to instantly evaporate one's self-confidence. This had in no way been the plan. I could feel my heart thundering somewhere in my chest, and my throat seemed to be getting tighter and tighter. Even the tiny piece of breadstick on his fork now seemed to be staring at me, watching for my next move. I felt paralysed. For the first time since someone told me that tonic water was fattening, I was completely and utterly floored.

But not for long. Even though I was fully aware that this was what getting your heart broken felt like, I was also most assuredly aware that if he was capable of talking to me like that, I was going to be better off without him in the long run. *Well*, that's not strictly true. I didn't really know it, but with the benefit of hindsight I reckon that on some kind of primal level, I was almost definitely slightly aware of it. In a women's intuition-type way. *Well*, perhaps there was a large part of me that had no idea that things would ever get any better. In fact, in all honesty, I think I can now remember how sure I was that nothing would ever, ever be good again. I was in complete shock – I think I mentioned that. This was not the plan. This was not the 'clearing the air' argument that I'd anticipated. This was most certainly not lusty debate that was ultimately going to bring us closer together, resulting in a realization a few short months later that we were ready to move in with each other. Instead, the only coping strategy springing to mind was to get up and leave the table. I am a firm believer that while running away won't solve your problems, it is often an excellent first move.

In short, there was no way I was going to stick around to eat my Pizza of Rejection. Nothing could convince me to sully my lips with such filth. Nate couldn't possibly want me to stay and eat. The waiters would just have to bring it to an empty table. So, with all the dignity I could muster while my bottom lip was wobbling, I stood up. Then reached into my bag and got out my credit card. I defiantly threw it on to the table as a gesture of utter contempt, knowing it wouldn't be used, but also knowing I was damned if I was going to be seen to accept his sympathy at this stage. Then, very slowly (and elegantly, I like to think), I walked to the bathroom. The minute I got there I realized that I didn't need the loo at all, and so the person in the stall next to me was going to think I was either quite mad, an unsubtle drug fiend or some kind of Rebecca Loos-type pervy textaholic. So I left the stall and stared blankly into the mirror, trying to work out how this had happened. It felt a little like a dream: when you wake up aware that you have experienced certain emotions, but the enormous unexplained gaps in your memory mean you have no idea how you came to be feeling these things. As I saw my as yet uncrying but nevertheless haggard face in the mirror, I understood how people like Simon Cowell got to be millionaires. All those songs, making all those promises about you never having to feel like this again, or how you're not alone because everyone has been through this at some stage. But I *was* alone. Alone in a strangely asymmetrical bathroom with slightly odd starey-looking eyes. Alone in the most intense way I had felt in my whole life.

My glazed eyes were starting to terrify me, and my bottom lip was quivering even more unnervingly. I could feel the tears – they weren't far off – so I decided it was time to get my belongings and leave as quickly as possible. I did not want him to see me crying. I left the bathroom, only slightly banging my face on the door as I pulled it open a little too fast, and only slightly staggering backwards as a result. I'm pretty sure no one saw me. I resumed my elegantly wounded but dignified walk back to the table. I was a couple of paces away when I realized two things: I now really did need the loo, and there were two credit card slips on the table. Yes, he'd dumped me. In public. And he'd gone Dutch. I was paying for my own Pizza of Rejection.

Luckily for me, my friend Sally was having a party

that night. Nate and I had been planning to go there after our pizza. I knew that at the very least I, as the wounded party, would keep custody of the night's social event, so I informed Nate that I was off to see Sally and that he wasn't welcome. He acknowledged defeat quickly (presumably relieved to be absolved of the responsibility for getting me home without incident) and walked with me to the tube stop. He then tried to kiss me goodbye, but I was concentrating too hard on getting away from him as briskly as possible so we ended up head-butting slightly and scuttling away in our different directions.

I'm sure you'll agree that apart from the whole my-argument-going-not-entirely-as-I'd-planned thing, I was doing pretty well. I'd been dumped, had so far maintained my dignity and, more importantly, was heading towards vodka and sympathy. Surely things could only get better. I was fine as I went down the escalator; I just tossed my hair back a few times, telling myself resolutely, 'Well, honestly, what a loser! He can't even come to Sally's party now, ha haa.' But then I had to wait seven minutes for a train, and the panic and sadness started to creep up on me. It was all starting to seem a little bleaker by the time the doors to my carriage opened.

As the train headed beneath the Thames, I had tears streaming down my face. There was no one in my carriage except a small oriental businessman who had so far ignored me studiously. A couple of seconds later I let out a huge, weird, gulpy sob. The businessman's head jerked up in shock, he caught my eye, looked as appalled as if I'd taken off all of my clothes to reveal buboes, and immediately looked away. I bowed my head and sniffed, willing the train to hurry up. I was the most humiliated I have ever been. And that's including the time I turned up for interviews at my prospective university on 14 March instead of 14 February.

On an ordinary day, the walk from the tube stop to Sally's party wouldn't have seemed too far – perhaps three or four minutes. But with a tear-stained, make-up-smeared face, a heart full of pain and a stomach full of nothing, the journey seemed interminable. I had managed some relatively effective damage control on the tear smears, using a paper napkin I had snuck into my pocket on leaving the restaurant, but it was the gulpy sobs I was most worried about. I shouldn't really have concerned myself with them; they were the least of my troubles, because for the last three hundred metres of the journey I'd been doing an extraordinary speed walk. So anxious was I to get myself to the bosom of my friends, I had adopted that loose-hipped yet competitive gait so beloved of Olympic walkers and pushy women on the first day of the Harrods sale. My dignified vignette was completed by my decision to try and hold my breath in order to stop myself from crying. So I had a puffed-out chest, a stained and blotchy face, *and* the walk of a constipated athlete.

And the promise of vodka.

As I opened the door to the pub I could immediately see Sally and James, Nate's best friend, standing on look-out for me, each armed with two vodka tonics.

'He texted us,' they said simultaneously, to which I thought simultaneously, How sweet, he just wants me to be OK. He still cares about me. Maybe we can work it all out tomorrow ... and, What a bloody saint, he'll spend 3p on a text to rid himself of the guilt of not having to look after me, but wouldn't fork out for my Pizza of Rejection. There then followed a delicate situation where my sobbing self tried to hug the two of them together while they still clutched a glass in each hand. We ended up resigning ourselves to a funny kind of chest-bump each, then settling down to The Explanation.

'So, what on earth brought it about? Why tonight? How did it happen?' demanded Sally.

'Well, we'd had a tiff on email earlier in the day because I was really upset with him after last night—'

'What happened last night? I saw you at the theatre and everything seemed fine,' interrupted James.

'He didn't come home with me, and then he didn't even call or text to check that I had got home OK. When I did get back to the flat and tried to call him, his phone was turned off because he'd already gone to bed. I wouldn't normally be such a wuss, and I know it's been a month since I was mugged, but what upset me was the idea that he could go to bed totally relaxed, not knowing if I was lying in a ditch or not.'

James nodded sagely as it dawned on him that immense disloyalty was now being required of him.

'Exactly, exactly,' Sally soothed. 'Well, it just goes to show that you're better off without him. The idiot, how could he be so selfish?' Sally was fast approaching her strident, no-nonsense stage of drunkenness. Usually this was quite exciting, as for 99 per cent of the time she is the very model of measured, reasoned behaviour and conversation. But when she feels strongly about something, there can be no predicting, no pattern and no containing the ways in which she might react. She can sit for entire dinner parties with a benign, pensive face, contributing the odd wry comment while everyone else starts to shame themselves with their bitching and giggling. Or she can start to giggle a lot, as if daring herself to say more and more uncharacteristically flippant things, until she's whipped herself into a sniggering frenzy usually reserved for young teenagers. Or, most excitingly of all, she can become Strident Sally.

And Strident Sally it was who got the full story of how I'd had the temerity to ask for a little support after getting mugged. I didn't expect a frickin' police escort, but a phone call at the end of the night would have been nice. At first it had been great going out with someone with so much respect for women, their strengths and their capabilities. But it turned out that Nate didn't seem to have quite so much respect for my frailties, and me prompting him had yielded unexpected results. This explanation was met with huffing and eye rolling from Sally (interspersed with a little hand squeezing and some hair stroking). James continued to nod sagely, and his loyalty stretched as far as: 'He just doesn't get it, does he?' This prompted further tears from me, and as soon as I had confirmation that my flatmate Jo was at home, ready for me, I tottered home.

I had always been under the impression that Jo was a huge fan of Nate. They'd got on when he was at our house or we were at mutual friends' parties, and she'd never really had a harsh word to say about him. But, as I opened the door to our little Shepherd's Bush flat that evening, I was quickly corrected. She was standing at the top of the stairs as I came in the outside door. Her hands were on her hips and her eyes were blazing. She had a packet of cigarettes sticking out of the front of her jeans like a loaded revolver. 'What a fucking wanker,' were her first words, and 'Do you want gin or vodka?' were her next. She was a great, great flatmate.

We stayed in the kitchen chatting for about an hour –

Jo pacing up and down, excelling herself with a varied and imaginative stream of obscenities and declarations, starting with the: 'Honestly, he wasn't all that. I mean, he had OK hair but he was a bit full of himself . . .' and working towards: 'The future begins now, and he is simply never going to feature in it!' via: 'Urgh, even his "cool" T-shirts made him look fat,' as I sat beneath a rug on the comfy kitchen chair shivering, laughing and sniffling.

I would love to be able to tell you that I then went to bed for some restful sleep before the hardship of the days to come. But I can't. I definitely went to bed. But then a couple of hours later I woke up. Vaguely aware that I felt a little melancholy about something, I shuffled over to the other side of the bed, seeking the heat of Nate's body to comfort me as I drifted back to sleep. And at this point I'd love to be able to tell you that I either a) realized my error, feistily tossed my long glossy hair across his pillow and went straight back to sleep dreaming of the success I was going to make of myself without him, or b) sat up, shed a delicate tear, lit a scented candle and did half an hour's meditation until I drifted back into heartbroken but elegant slumber. But I can't.

It's a long time ago now, so I've pretty much shrugged off most of the shame, but the truth was this: I woke up, rolled over, remembered what had happened and burst into tears like an irrational five-year-old who has just realized she's lost a mitten at the play park. I was inconsolable. I had gone to bed relatively positive after Jo's excellent impression of the evil renegade member of a desperate girl group. But all of a sudden it was 3.30 a.m., I was all alone, I felt rather shaky (possibly DTs after what must have been half a bottle of vodka?) and it was all coming flooding back. I burst into bizarre howling tears and sat on my bed crying for about twenty minutes before I decided to have a bath, where I sat, shoulders still heaving, thick ropes of snot coming out of my nose, for a further twenty minutes. At a couple of points I actually got a bit bored of the fact that I was still crying, and tried some variations on the common bawl in the hope that Jo might wake up and carry on feeling sorry for me. Unfortunately she'd had the other half of the bottle of vodka and was fast asleep sounding alarmingly like Grandpa Simpson. Then a new wave would hit me and I just surrendered, hoping that perhaps I could get all of the hurt out in one batch and then be fine by morning, kind of like cash-and-carry heartache. Eventually, after an extended spell of the weird stuttery breathing you get after a serious bout of crying, I got myself together, back into bed and back to sleep.

The next morning I was woken by what I initially thought was my alarm clock but turned out to be my mobile phone ringing. It was my sister Lily. Despite being three years younger, Lily is infinitely better than me at most things that matter. The most obvious of her effortless talents are her looks. While I struggled through my teens, unappetizingly combining puppy fat with eighties fashion, Lily preferred to glide through adolescence, the kind of terrifying teenager who exudes a disdainful cool. I was just about coming to terms with her superior cool skills when I invited her to come and stay with me at university, only for the guy I'd had my eye on all term to declare: 'Lily's gorgeous, she looks just like a digitally enhanced version of you.' I had slipped past the finishing post of life's early challenges, such as riding a bike with stabilizers, mastering Latin grammar or tying the laces on a pair of GreenFlash, but Lily has always been a fountain of knowledge on anything actually useful – driving, sales shopping, being able to stand up to your boss or, indeed, negotiating with boys.

She's also a firm believer in telling it like it is. Sometimes she doesn't even bother with telling it like it *actually* is, but just goes for how she'd *like* it to be. Thus, she seems to make things go her way.

'Oh, Ali, I got your text when I woke up. How are you?'

'Um, OK, I suppose. Where are you? Can you talk?'

'Yes, I'm outside of work, waiting for them to open up, but I've been here for ten minutes and no one's turned up. Idiots.'

Lily used to work for a flagship branch of Gap, where she managed to exceed every sales target she was ever set through sheer force of personality and belief in the fact that she knew what made people look their best. Innocents would come in for a pair of socks and leave with complete new wardrobes, as well as entirely fresh perspectives on themselves.

Having been told the basics, it didn't take her long to launch into her opinion on what had gone wrong in my relationship. She believed that the rot had set in years ago. Unfortunately for me, she also believed in telling me so, truthfully and brutally.

'You know, every guy isn't automatically going to dump you and you've got to get your head around that. Also, you're not actually the first person that this has happened to. And as for Nate, you've been moaning about the things he's done for ages. What on earth stopped you from seeing it coming?'

'Well, now that you put it like that, I don't know really. I guess I must just be really stupid.'

'Oh, get a grip! What are you talking about? You know Latin and loads of stuff about old books. Surely you can handle *this*, you little git.'

'Well, what good are books? What the hell is the point in knowing fucking Latin if I'm still so crushingly idiotic about boys? I feel as if I'm the only person dumb enough to have ever been dumped, and I feel as if no one will ever understand how painful this is. I can physically feel it.'

'Don't be so bloody ridiculous. It's happened to the best of us.'

'That doesn't matter to me. It's not making it any better or worse to know that it's happened to almost everyone. It feels like the first time. And I feel like I'm the only one.'

'For heaven's sake – you're not.'

I was beginning to regret seeking any kind of solace in sisterhood, as she seemed to be using it as some kind of excuse to remind me that I was a massive nerd and she has been cool since she was a zygote. She could be so selfish. 'Well, who's been dumped as painfully as me? WHO?'

'I've got my own life to live, you know? I don't have time to indulge you like this. You shouldn't dwell on these things when you could be doing something sensible like Scottish Country Dancing instead . . .'

'Something sensible like Scottish Country Dancing?! You're going to be opening village fêtes next. What *are* you talking about?'

'Everyone knows it's the thing that makes you happiest,

because it involves the four key elements to contentment: interaction with others, physical exercise, music and a sense of flow that makes you concentrate on patterns. It's really very cheering.'

'You're crazy. I am NOT going to start dancing.'

'Fine. But you'll wish you had. And you still won't be the only person to have ever been dumped. I know you like to think you're special, but you're not alone in this one.'

'*I'm* the one who likes to think *she's* special?'

'Zip it, sista.'

2

You're Nobody 'Til Somebody Dumps You: The Heartbroken in History

Don't get the idea that I'm one to wallow in the misery of my fellow sisters (I can't think how you would), but it's a sorry fact that we all risk the pain of being dumped. It turns out it's happened to the best and the worst of us. In fact, it usually happens to the strongest, coolest and most beautiful women imaginable – because they're the ones who are brave enough to be emotional risk-takers, or are simply the ones who scare men a little bit with their mighty feminine prowess.

Whatever you do, don't look at this as a list of examples of how to respond to getting dumped. Not all of these women dealt with the situation admirably. They can offer some lessons, but most of all they offer comfort; it's good to know that it's been happening since the dawn of time and continues to happen – Kylie is testament to this fact – and you are not alone in suffering this pain.

Dido – Queen of Carthage, star of the Latin text
The Aeneid by Virgil, published in 19 BC

Let's kick off with Dido, as, quite frankly, she was a mega-star – gorgeous, powerful, and more than a little feisty . . .

As with most powerful women, Dido had a reputation for being high maintenance. As with most powerful women . . . NO WONDER! For heaven's sake, at a young age she was married to her uncle, who was then murdered for his cash by her brother. Instead of staying in and watching reruns of ancient Greek *Sex and the City* she went off and founded a city of her own – by the niftiest means imaginable. Iarbas, a local king, took a shine to her and said he'd give her as much land as could be covered by a single ox hide. Instead of swooning with either gratitude or indignation, she rolled her eyes, rolled her sleeves up and had a hide cut into strips then stretched. Hence Carthage. And she didn't even have to snog Iarbas!

He wrought his mighty revenge (as they did) in his

own way. When Aeneas, a travelling Trojan soldier, found himself on the shores of Carthage, it wasn't long before he and Dido were exchanging furtive glances and Dido was confessing her crush to her sister Anna. It turned out that even property-savvy royalty have hearts: she could 'get no peace from love's disquiet', and as they were doing their eyeliner-heavy make-up and twirly Greek hairstyles Dido was soon exclaiming: 'How gallantly he looks! How powerful in chest and shoulders! I really do think, and have reason to think, that he is heaven-born.' She had it bad.

Anna quite rightly told her to go for it, but as one with a somewhat forthright sister myself, I do think it was a little harsh of her to describe Dido's heart as 'atrophying'. Up in the heavens Juno and Venus – very much the Sharon Osbourne and Dermot O'Leary of mortal love affairs – decided to Make It So. The next day Dido and Aeneas had planned a grand day's hunting, and while they were out in the woods, the gods got to work on an epic storm. And what do you know? Soon they found themselves sheltering in the same cave, and it didn't take too long before one thing led to another . . .

The new couple, looking an awful lot like Kate and Sawyer from *Lost*, went on to 'spend the winter in debauchery'. It was surely an inevitability that Iarbus would soon find out, and when he did he went straight to Jupiter – the Simon Cowell of the gods. You see, Aeneas had a previous deal with Jupiter (to found Rome and to do so without dallying in Carthage), so he had to dump the lovely Dido. That most ancient of conversations ensued: 'I have to concentrate on my career right now. This next year or so is when I've really got to make my mark, and I can't fully commit to a full-on relationship at the moment.'

'Great, tell me this now that I've totally fallen in love with you, exposed my most intimate thoughts and emotions to you, and spent the winter in debauchery with you.'

Aeneas was perhaps the first in a long line of men to top it off with, 'Well, I never promised to marry you either, did I?' (For the geeks among you, the Latin for this is: *'nec coniugis umquam praetendi taedas, aut haec in foedera veni.'*)

Dido tried everything to get Aeneas to stay. Don't we all. She even developed 'hectic blotches upon her quivering cheeks' – it's a relief to know I'm not the only one that happens to. Unfortunately she went a little off-message at this point, and hurled herself onto an enormous pyre and stabbed herself with a sword Aeneas (the old romantic) had given her.

Poor old Dido had a tough life and an even harsher

end. I like to think that if I'd been around I could have had a good go at talking her round. Perhaps Anna wasn't as good a sister as Lily. Or maybe I'm just lucky I've never had to go up against Jupiter for a man. Either way, the story of Dido and Aeneas is hugely comforting – if it can happen to someone as cool as Dido then it can happen to anyone.

There are few women who know as much about heartache as **Miss Piggy.** There are even fewer pigs. But none of them handle it with such verve and élan.

'Is there a cure for a broken heart? Only time can heal your broken heart, just as only time can heal his broken arms, legs . . .' Miss Piggy

Jennifer Aniston – actor and ex-Mrs Pitt

I can't imagine that there's much more to be said about Jennifer Aniston's heinous celebrity dumping by Brad Pitt, but it is worth remembering that there were ten whole years when a large number of us wished we could be her, before she unwillingly donned her crown as The World's Most Famous Dumpee.

From the moment that *Friends* hit our screens Rachel Green – and by extension Jennifer Aniston – was the cute, funny girl who could persuade guys to do whatever she wanted. She was the infuriating girl who got effortlessly served first at the bar, and didn't have to pay speeding fines because she made the traffic policeman think that he actually had a chance with her. For years we wanted Jen's hair, Jen's fun job, Jen's wardrobe-to-die-for, and Jen's perfect marriage.

In those days Angelina was just a scary goth with big lips and a crush on her brother – no one really took her that seriously. But then Angelina had a swift transformation into some kind of Mother Earth/Audrey Hepburn hybrid and began her full schedule of adopting babies like other people collect different-coloured Smartie lids. All of a sudden Angelina was kind, wise and beautiful, while Jennifer was slightly lightweight, with silly high-maintenance hair and a visible neediness that was miles from Uber-Angelina's apparent competence. And she was dumped. As is ever the case, that which had once made her so vulnerable, so lovable, was now her downfall.

There are those who like to nod their heads wisely, talking slowly and meaningfully about the vacuous celebrity culture we live in today, and how the tabloids reduce everything to over-simplified soap operas. Then there are those, like me, who think, OH MY GOD! If you can have THAT MUCH going for you and you can *still* get dumped, then what hope is there for the rest of us?

Jennifer is notoriously reticent with the press, but did give one revealing interview to *Vanity Fair* magazine where she slyly said of Brad that 'there's a sensitivity chip that's missing'. Delicately put. But the most intriguing thing about the interview was that while she never actually conceded to Brad having an affair with Angelina while they were still married, she was more than happy to admit that she had effectively been dumped. She was emphatic that she'd wanted to make it work, to have babies and devote herself to him, come what may, but that she hadn't been afforded the opportunity. In today's world of celebrity 'exhaustion' and 'amicable splits' this is rare honesty for a celebrity. The world was so happy that it wasn't just them getting dumped that Jen immediately became a poster girl for the lovelorn across the globe.

Better yet, in that *Vanity Fair* article Jennifer admitted that the only way that she could cope with the relentless press scrutiny was to wear 'an imaginary dog cone, so I don't see anything. It just allows for a much more peaceful life.' I can't help thinking that while it's a nifty tip to wear an imaginary dog cone when you're in the harshest early stages of a break-up, it would be considerably more cheering to imagine someone as poised as Jennifer Aniston wearing hers. I can't believe there's a heartache out there that couldn't be punctured just for a minute by that image.

> Award-winning novelist **Lionel Shriver**, author of *We Need to Talk About Kevin*, recently answered the question 'Have you ever been dumped?' in a newspaper interview with: '*Numerous times. Thankfully. A far more vital rite of passage than losing your cherry is having it squashed under some cad's heel.*'
>
> I bet she even holds the hair back of her freshly dumped friends when they're sick after an evening of excessive white wine and 'plenty more fish in the sea'-ing.

Giselle – star of the romantic ballet based on Nordic myth, originally choreographed by Jean Coralli and Jules Perrot, and first performed in 1841

I can't lie to you. There is very little to learn from the story of Giselle. It is clearly one of the most ludicrous tales ever told. But it's about getting dumped and seeking revenge – and I have a dream that one day it will be updated and set in the Bronx starring Jennifer Lopez, so I thought I should include it anyway.

Giselle is an innocent young girl who lives in a small village in Germany. She is very pure and innocent, as well as having a rather weak heart. Something of a Marissa Cooper, as played by Mischa Barton in *The OC*. The story starts on the day of the village's annual grape harvest festivities, where there is much dancing and merriment. As well as being innocent and delicate to the point of tedium, she is a high-spirited girl and enjoys the dancing that the evening entails. Her mother warns her to take it easy though, on account of her prophetically weak heart.

At the grape harvest she meets and falls in love with the dashing Prince Albrecht, who, in the manner of Prince Harry, is wearing a disguise. Instead of being dressed like a Nazi he is masquerading as a peasant, in order to get down with the kids without the paparazzi in his face. Albrecht too falls deeply in love with Giselle but, being entirely perfect in every single way, Giselle resists his advances until she is sure of this trustworthiness and fidelity. Unfortunately, it transpires that she's not quite as clever as she thought, as Hilarion, the local gamekeeper who has long had designs on her, reveals that in fact Albrecht is already engaged to gorgeous Princess Bathilde. Unable to take such a cruel blow to her delicate self-confidence and rickety heart, Giselle promptly kills herself. I cannot stress enough how much I do not approve of this.

But now the story momentarily becomes fun. Giselle is buried in the woods, where she becomes one of the ghostly Willis. Yes, the ghostly Willis. The Willis are the spirits of local girls who have died, betrayed by their loved ones, and for revenge they lure men into the forest only to dance them to death. (Can you *imagine* how fabulous an updated version of this story would be? JLo's dance breakdowns which feature in almost every one of her pop videos are terrifying enough, but imagine if she were actually dancing someone to death. Through the backstreets of New York. Set in about 1978. Seriously, I think someone should take this on.)

Anyway, poor faithful Hilarion wanders into the forest to mourn Giselle, only to be spotted by Myrtha, Queen of the Willis (possibly to be played by Madonna in my version), and promptly danced to death. On the other hand, when Albrecht arrives in the forest shortly afterwards, he is protected by Giselle, who is still doolally with love for him and beats the Willis in a dance-off, saving the life of stupid two-timing Albrecht.

While this is a beautiful ballet to look at, and the floaty fairies in wedding dresses mournfully tottering about on their toes are the stuff of little girls' dreams, I can't help thinking that Giselle is rather wet, completely misguided and not nearly as perfect as she thinks she is. While my remake would be considerably feistier, I suppose the best we can learn from her story is that you can be *too* nice. And that dancing boys to death is probably quite good fun if you like that kind of thing.

Wuthering Heights – Kate Bush and Emily Brontë

Most people assume that poor old Catherine is horribly dumped by the brooding Heathcliff in Emily Brontë's novel, but in fact it never actually happens. I am assuming we all think this because everyone quite rightly remembers her in some form of anguish or another throughout the story. Also, because Kate Bush's iconic song had Cathy wondering how he could leave her when she needed 'to possess' him and has the poor girl outside in the cold, begging to be let in for a cup of Ovaltine. She later resorts to threats about grabbing his soul away.

I am not sure about much, but I am certain that this kind of comment is not a good way to keep a boyfriend. What does take place in the actual novel is an epic degree of volatile emotions, paranoia, eavesdropping and misunderstandings. It's basically like a really, really bad episode of *The Sopranos* set on the Yorkshire moors when all the gangsters have crippling PMS.

Perhaps I wouldn't boast about it to someone I fancied, but I will never have a bad word said about the song. It's just so mind-blowingly bonkers. Seriously, if you've ever been made to feel like a hysterical woman by some patronizingly rational boyfriend, don't sit around trying to hold it in – get it out! Go for a long walk and listen to 'Wuthering Heights' on your iPod. Really loud. And then sing along. It's soooo satisfying. (I've heard.)

Ariadne – star of Greek myth, written ages ago by lots of different poets who couldn't quite get their stories straight

Ariadne's dumping at the hands of Theseus was harsh, to say the very least. But it was also very dramatic, on account of the frankly farcical family politics involved. I'd like you, if you would, to imagine this story as a big-budget TV show, possibly directed by Aaron Spelling, creator of shows such as *Dynasty*, *Melrose Place* and *Beverly Hills 90210*. Let me explain.

Theseus was a right stud, and son of Aegeus, King of Athens to boot. He wasn't a lad without problems, though. I'm not entirely sure what parenting manuals

Aegeus read, but his fathering skills were erratic at best. When Aegeus found out his wife was pregnant, he took her to a town outside of Athens, hid a sword and a pair of sandals under a very heavy rock, then headed back to Athens announcing that his future child (Theseus) was only to come and visit him once he was strong enough to lift the rock and get the (presumably crushed) sandals 'n' sword kit. Theseus was only sixteen by the time he could do this, and he began his trek to Athens, his now long blond hair billowing behind him in the breeze, along with the trail of villains he had slain en route.

Unfortunately, the father–son bonding did not go as planned, because Aegeus had married the evil and incessantly plotting Medea in the intervening sixteen years, and she was determined to get rid of her pesky stepson Theseus. There was further hindrance to their special bonding on account of the fact that the Athenians had somehow got themselves in some ancient-world version of a bad franchise deal with the local islanders, the Cretans. It seems to have been quite a costly transaction, as their side of the bargain was to send seven Athenian girls and seven Athenian boys to Crete each year to be killed by the Minotaur.

The Minotaur was Ariadne's half-brother. Nothing wrong with unconventional family dynamics, I hear you say. But I can't help feeling queasy about the fact that the Minotaur was half-man, half-bull – the result of Ariadne's mother Pasiphae sleeping with a bull. Now that's a family secret – no wonder they kept him in a labyrinth in the cellar and only used him for eating Athenians. But it wasn't strictly Pasiphae's fault; the god Poseidon had sent her husband Minos (Ariadne's dad) a perfect white bull for sacrificial purposes, but Minos sneakily kept it for breeding. The result of this, um, beef, was an altogether unanticipated kind of breeding: Poseidon made Pasiphae fall in love with the bull and even got a cow costume made for her to wear while, well, doing 'it'. This is something that even Alexis Colby never stooped to.

Somewhat predictably, Theseus – presumably in a desperate bid to finally get some attention from his frankly rather self-absorbed father – offered to be one of the seven young men sent off to Crete. His master plan was to prove that he was 'one of the guys' (a bit like when Prince William is allowed to talk to footballers) and to somehow kill the Minotaur. On arrival, it didn't take long for Theseus' broad shoulders, gleaming hair and can-do attitude to entrance the lovely Ariadne, who quickly offered to help him evade her monstrous half-brother. Her plan was simple but effective. She gave Theseus a sword and a ball of string to use as a guide as he wound his way through the labyrinth, thus enabling him to defeat the poor old Minotaur *and* find his way out again. Still high on his victory, Theseus scooped Ariadne into his capable arms, promised her marriage and headed home for Athens, stopping on the way for a break on the island of Naxos.

Theseus seems to have had a moment of clarity one day on Naxos, and realized that now he was a bona fide hero he could have any girl he wanted and didn't have to make do with the one from a freaky family to whom he owed a favour. In the long tradition of rock stars and footballers who suddenly hit the big time, he suddenly abandoned Ariadne. Literally. She woke up one morning to find herself all alone on the island. This has to rate pretty highly on the extreme-dumping scale. To be emotionally abandoned is one thing, and usually leaves you feeling like you've been stranded on a desert island anyway, but to be physically abandoned as well must have been tough. It goes to show, you always get dumped just when you think everything's going to turn out just fine.

The Latin poet Catullus beautifully channels her mood at this point, and is extremely sympathetic to the plight of the recently dumped woman. He vividly describes her violent emotional yo-yoing from: 'I must be reunited with you whatever it takes. I simply cannot live without you, even if it means sneaking into Athens as your servant . . .' to 'I never, ever want to see or hear of you again, and am actively repulsed by the level of servitude I have already shown you.'

At this point, there are two different versions of how Ariadne's story ends. The lesser known one is that Artemis, the hunting goddess, sees how gutted Ariadne is and kills her to put her out of her pain. It should go without saying that I'm not keen on this ending, particularly as I felt so let down by Dido and Giselle's attitude to being dumped. Artemis was not a terribly intuitive woman – perhaps she'd never been dumped at this early stage before, and didn't understand how quickly you start to feel better.

While I'm not entirely in favour of the tactic of replacing your ex as quickly as possible, this is the second version of how Ariadne's story ends. I suppose we should cut her a little slack – everyone deserves to be made to feel like a goddess. In her new man, the god Dionysus, she found someone who treated her with the respect she deserved and actually did make her a goddess. They stayed together on Naxos drinking fine ouzo and eating tasty feta cheese, oblivious to the fate of Theseus and his pathetic attempts to get Daddy's attention. Indeed, it turns out he was rather more flustered by his break-up with Ariadne than he would like to have let on, because he forgot to change sails on his ship – a highly significant mistake. As he sailed triumphantly into the harbour of Athens, his ship was still displaying black sails, indicating that he had been killed on his expedition. On seeing this signal his father Aegeus hurled himself off the harbour's cliff top in grief, killing himself instantly. Let that be a lesson to those who scarper in the middle of the night.

It's such a shame that **Maria Callas** was born when she was – thirty years later and she would be a massive reality TV star, healing the pain with fabulous, catchily named shows like *How to Handle Heartache Like a Diva.*

Born in the 1920s she was a huge opera star by the 1950s, famed for both her voice and her acting skills. In 1954 she gave herself a dramatic image overhaul, losing a huge amount of weight and becoming quite the glamour-puss. Shortly afterwards, she attracted the attentions of Greek shipping billionaire and international playboy Aristotle Onassis, and went on to leave her poor husband for him. Theirs was the first truly tabloid romance, and kept tongues wagging across Europe and the US (although I'll wager a lot of the talk was about the bizarre jumpsuit patterned with enormous cabbage roses that she famously wore when on board Onassis's luxury yacht, the *Christina*).

The pair were Greek superstars flaunting their love to the world, and living it up Puff Daddy and Jennifer Lopez-style long before bling was invented. All this came to a sudden halt when Onassis abruptly left Maria for uptight, recently widowed and beautifully shod gold-digger Jackie Kennedy. As Maria admitted: 'First I lost my voice, then I lost my figure and then I lost Onassis.'

She was a stylish and imperious diva until the end, though, and resisted flinging herself at either swords or unsuitable men. Paris Hilton has recently revived the fashion for dating Greek shipping billionaires, but with no voice and little spare weight to lose, her efforts have been characteristically shoddy, to say the least. But if she ever gets a cabbage rose jumpsuit, things might change . . .

Buffy – star of the US TV show by Joss Whedon

It's no coincidence that television was invented in the same decade as the teenager. They were made for each other, and since they have both existed there has never been a shortage of teen dramas on air. But few have had the wit, the passion or the heart of *Buffy the Vampire Slayer*. Admittedly the rest got off on the back foot as they didn't have a butt-kicking sixteen-year-old whose destiny it was to save the world as their heroine. Buffy didn't just go to school, snog boys, put on some lipgloss and then waffle on about it to her mates – she went to school, snogged boys, put on some lipgloss, then went out all night to slay the vampires terrorizing the Californian town of Sunnydale. The genius of the show is that every teenager genuinely believes that they are the most important person in the world, and that every problem they have or emotion they feel could quite possibly affect the lives of everyone on the planet. So, when Buffy got dumped – an event which did actually affect the lives of others – a generation of teenagers (and I, who was twenty-six at the time and newly dumped) nodded their heads sagely in understanding.

Buffy's boyfriend is Angel, a 200-year-old vampire with a soul, who is very kind, very gentle and loves her dearly. The only impediment to their true love (other than her mother, who thinks – quite reasonably, given his looks – he's nineteen and therefore too old for her) is the small issue of a gypsy curse. He gets to have a soul and be good but he must also be for ever tormented by guilt for the crimes he committed when he was an evil vampire. And if ever he experiences 'a moment of true happiness' (i.e. sex!) the curse will break, returning him to his evil form. It's just that Buffy doesn't know this. So, when things begin to get hot and heavy between the Californian corn-fed creatures of the night, and Buffy starts to use every teenager's justification for losing her virginity – 'But what if I never feel this way again?' – we know that sex can only end in disaster for the residents of Sunnydale.

Sure enough, one thing leads to another on the night of Buffy's seventeenth birthday, and what follows is one of the cruellest dumpings in television history. Buffy wakes up the next morning to find Angel gone and her head a jumble of conflicting emotions. To make matters worse, her mother immediately notices that she 'looks different'. The horror! When Angel finally does turn up, he is every first-timer's worst nightmare – initially pretending to have forgotten that anything of Huge Significance occurred between them the night before, then implying that it had all been rather tedious, before finally accusing her of being a bit of a slut for giving it up so easily. This is the triple whammy of agony and insult that every teenage girl – indeed every girl – fears the most when they get close to a guy. Although, looking on the bright side, at no stage does Angel criticize the bizarre giraffe-print leggings she had been wearing that fateful evening. Small mercies.

After this brutal treatment and her initial stupor, Buffy realizes that her love life has set Armageddon in motion, and that she needs to get her act together. In spite of her mother's protestations that 'it's not as if breaking up with Angel is the end of the world or anything', and despite the palpable bafflement of her bumbling British mentor Giles at what could possibly have made Angel turn evil, Buffy allows herself only a brief moment of weeping before doing some light stretching and then heading off into the night to do what must be done: execute Angel. While I know we all feel we'd like to do that at moments, you've got to feel for the girl, and admire her awesome recovery skills.

Madame Butterfly, opera by Giacomo Puccini, first performed in 1904

Having exhausted myself with my disapproval of Giselle and her response to being dumped, I can barely bring myself to tell you the story of *Madame Butterfly*. To cut an appalling story short, Ms Butterfly is a fifteen-year-old geisha who falls in love with Lieutenant Pinkerton, an American sailor working in Japan. She marries him, renouncing her family and her religion, only for him to be called back to his ship and depart for three years.

Somewhat predictably he goes off and finds himself a lovely new American wife. To make matters worse, he doesn't even let Butterfly know. On his return to Japan he is too cowardly to confront his first wife, and leaves it to Kate, his second, to do the dirty work. Butterfly agrees to leave them her daughter and kills herself.

The opera is very beautiful and I'm sure the sets often look splendid, but this 'If I can't have you, life is not worth living' attitude is really beginning to get to me. Forgive me if I sound like a teacher, but I am the Queen of Dumped and in this instance I do know best. Suicide is NO WAY to behave, just because you've had your heart broken. You know this, and I know this. Don't do it. Things get better. Vastly.

Honestly, the only explanation for this shoddy response to heartache is either a) 'I Will Survive' would not make a good opera, or b) A man wrote it. I am even slightly convinced that there is a secret fourth act written by Mrs Puccini, where it turns out that Madame Butterfly was just having a kip before hatching an amazing plan to go to Texas to become a property magnate and part-time pottery expert.

Minnie Driver – actress and musician

While we're on the subject of making a kerfuffle, for almost a decade it has been widely reported that in 1998 Minnie Driver was the recipient of both an Oscar nomination (for *Good Will Hunting*) and one of the most public dumpings in Hollywood history. The story goes that Matt Damon, her co-star and then boyfriend, gave a pre-Oscar interview to Oprah Winfrey, during which he unceremoniously announced that he and Minnie were no longer an item – having neglected to let Minnie know this first. If true, the boy deserved not only an Oscar for cruelty but also a big slap from Ms Winfrey.

Minnie gave several interviews subtly supporting rumours of this nefarious deed, describing his behaviour as 'fantastically inappropriate'. She turned up sporting a Very Brave Face and Defiant Red Dress to the Oscars ceremony itself – which Matt attended with his box-fresh new girlfriend, Winona Ryder. However, in the last few years, the story seems to have been clarified a little. Minnie's sister Kate admitted in a *Cosmo* interview that the couple had broken up before the Oprah episode, and Damon himself has now given several interviews (emphatically) confirming this fact.

What no one can take away from Driver is that she was dumped for Ryder. Ouch, especially as Matt went very public with Winona very quickly – and not only is she jaw-droppingly beautiful but, um, a little bit loopy, which must have irritated someone as self-possessed as Minnie. Her fury about it being announced on *Oprah* is understandable, even if she had been told in advance. But Driver's current public image as the girl who got dumped, made a big fuss and then turned out not to be that big a star, provides a lesson here for us all: the moral high ground might seem comfy and warm, but make sure your facts are straight before you get there, or you might find yourself stuck there for ever. And it must be chilly up there by yourself.

The very same **Winona Ryder** recently endeared herself to the heartbroken all over the world when she admitted that she'd been 'embarrassingly over-dramatic' when she broke up with Johnny Depp. My initial reaction on reading this comment was 'How dramatic is over-dramatic if it's Johnny Depp you've just broken up with – after four years? For heaven's sake, look at the lasting damage he did to Kate Moss's taste in men.' But then Winona went on to admit that she 'attempted being an alcoholic for two weeks, spending a lot of time in my hotel room, drinking screwdrivers from the minibar, smoking cigarettes and listening to endless Tom Waits'. OK, so that is pretty over-dramatic. But it's still to be encouraged, in my opinion, if only to make me feel better.

Scarlett O'Hara – heroine of Margaret Mitchell's *Gone With the Wind*

Ladies, as an antidote to some of that lily-livered behaviour from the likes of Ms Butterfly, Ms Driver and Ms Giselle, may I present you with the ultimate in resilient dumpees: Miss Scarlett O'Hara. A person my grandmother would have called 'One of life's bouncers', this girl deserved much of what she got, but still came back fighting. And looking gorgeous.

Scarlett begins the novel (and the film) completely unable to comprehend the idea that there might be a man on earth who wouldn't want her, and quite rightly sees how 'a pretty dress and a clear complexion are weapons to vanquish fate'. When her faithful maid Mammy disapproves of her choice of dress because 'you kain show yo' buzzum befo' three o'clock', she sees this as a challenge and promptly wears it to a barbecue, where she understandably attracts the attention of every man there. Well, almost every man there – she quickly learns that life isn't quite as simple as flashing your ankles (or anything else) at the one to whom you've taken a shine. The gentleman she has her eye on has set his sights on the rather wishy-washy Melanie, and has proposed to her. There is absolutely no lungeing onto swords or whingeing to the press from Scarlett at this point – she simply throws a vase at a wall, flirts with Rhett Butler and snaffles another man in the form of Charles, Melanie's brother, whom she goes on to marry.

Charles dies before long, leaving Scarlett to spend most of the rest of the story not grieving, but bouncing between Rhett (clearly an early incarnation of *Sex and the City*'s Mr Big) and Ashley (Aidan). Ashley is quite pathetic and never really manages to do the right thing, despite constantly purporting to be being led by the desire to be 'good'. He is clearly mesmerized by Scarlett, and almost always bends to her will – be it telling her he loves her, going to war or randomly setting up a lumber business. It's pretty obvious that his attraction to her is the mixture of almost complete subservience combined with the lustre of unattainability – a heady combination, wouldn't you agree, Ms Bradshaw?

Nevertheless, it is Rhett who is the real hero of the story. He can see right through Scarlett's wily ways, he lets himself be cruelly hurt by her, but clearly adores her despite her erratic behaviour, which ranges from scandalously dancing with him while still mourning her first husband and later trying to con him into giving money to revive her family's cotton plantation, to riding her buggy through the Shanty town and causing a right commotion. At one point she dresses up in some old curtains to snag a rich husband. It's worth bearing in mind that this is also a technique used to great effect by Maria in *The Sound of Music*. Gold-diggers, take note – your home furnishings could be your greatest asset.

There are those who believe that Scarlett simply gets what she deserves in the end, but I'm more of the opinion that she simply does what she has to in order to survive, and that some of her methods are just a little . . . over-imaginative. It's clear all along that Rhett is whom she should be with, but that she's not going to settle down until she's got some excess feistiness out of her system. Which is why his final 'My dear, I don't give a damn' is so devastating – we know she truly loves him.

The final page describes the sensation of just being dumped almost perfectly:

There was a merciful dullness in her mind, a dullness that she knew from long experience would soon give way to a sharp pain, even as severed tissues, shocked by the surgeon's knife, have a brief moment of insensibility before their agony begins.

But instead of giving up, scrabbling after him or resorting to a ludicrous dance-off, she brushes herself down, raises her chin, and announces that she'll 'think of it all tomorrow. After all, tomorrow is another day.'

If only someone had told Giselle.

3

The First Twenty-Four Hours

Getting dumped is grim. But there's something particularly awful about the way that life just carries on around you after it's happened. No one's noticed your entire life has swung on its axis: the world continues to turn, the stuff to do keeps mounting up, and the bills still have to be paid. Disgraceful. But there was absolutely no way that I could avoid the office that hideous day, as I had to spend much of it with an important client. Had someone asked me what I absolutely did not want to have to do that day, I don't think I would have thought of the answer: 'I'm really not keen on the idea of having to accompany Larry Hagman, aka *Dallas*'s J.R. Ewing, to a series of promotional interviews. Yes, I know he's a TV legend, and I'm sure he's a lovely man, but I simply don't think I'm the girl for the job today.'

But I *was* that girl. That was my job. I couldn't hide in bed until I stopped feeling as if every man, woman and child were whispering: 'She's the one that got dumped – again!' as I passed them in the street. I had to get up and drag myself to my desk. Urgh. And as with all such monstrous days, there were very specific items of clothing that were going to have to get me through it. No, not a Stetson. Nor the man-sized T-shirt that I stole from him. My garment of choice was an altogether different prospect. It was an old jumper that was by now barely smart enough to wear to work, but was just about passable if worn beneath a smart coat. The fabric was unexceptional, it didn't look particularly classy on, and it wasn't given to me by a beloved special one. But, on account of my own idiocy, it had become the jumper that made me more relaxed than any other item of clothing I owned.

You see, I had bought that sky-blue jumper for the first day at my job three years earlier. A special treat, something to feel comfortable in when I was nervous in my new, more senior role. The only trouble was that when I put it on that first day, I felt terribly uncomfortable for the entire time I was wearing it. Not just uncomfortable in that I didn't feel I looked my best – I actually felt almost strangulated. It was horrific. I couldn't even put my arms forward to rest on the desk in my first marketing meeting, as I could hardly breathe. I knew I'd bought the right size, so for the whole day my mind was a whirlwind of worries. For the entire time I was being shown the photocopying room and getting introduced to the team in the post room I was worrying that I had somehow gained two stone in a week. By the end of the marketing meeting I was convinced that my body was having some kind of primal reaction to my working in a larger, more corporate company. It wasn't until I returned home at the end of the day and went to take off the wretched thing that I realized I'd been wearing the jumper back to front all day. It wasn't the realities of a more responsible working role inducing the terrible feeling of suffocation – it was the yoke seams of my jumper. So, once I'd turned it around, that jumper felt like the most comfortable, indeed liberating, item of clothing I could ever wish to posses.

Having grabbed the Jumper of Strangulation from my cupboard, I managed to get myself washed, dressed and almost tolerably groomed, and intrepidly made my ten stops on the tube without frightening anyone with gulpy sobs. Pretty good. I was gaining a little confidence. Perhaps heartache wasn't going to fell me as if I were a spindly sapling after all. There was even a hint of a defiant swagger in my walk as I headed towards my office building. But then memory played a cruel trick. Just as I passed the doors to the building, admiring the elegant marble of the foyer as I entered, I had a sudden visual memory of Nate and me standing hand in hand outside the building. It felt as if I'd seen a ghost. I remembered the two of us going on our Sunday afternoon walk through Covent Garden all that time ago. We'd been to find the building so that I wouldn't get lost on my first day in my new job, and so that he'd be able to visualize where I was when he emailed me in my office. How could that have been him? How could someone that thoughtful be the same person who had now chewed me up, spat me out and ground me into the crowded pavement like a stick of discarded chewing gum? Because he'd been thoughtful a lot of the time. That's why I'd fallen so madly in love with him. Oh God, perhaps it was just me who had managed to turn that off in him.

As the lift doors closed, I felt my entire body slump, as if someone had snipped the tendons from behind my knees. By the time the doors opened at my floor I was only able to keep the sobs down by holding my breath. Fresh tears were perched on the edges of my eyelids like a pair of eager puddles.

The walk from the lift to my office was probably about twenty metres, but it felt like the length of Regent Street. With my breath held, my knees still more than a little unreliable, and the magical powers of my jumper nothing but a distant memory, I hobbled to my office, breaking into an Olympic-speed wobble towards the end. I hurled myself through my office door and slammed it behind me. With that, I cried, shaking all the while like a wet dog, for a good three or four minutes. Until I realized that I wasn't alone.

I don't want you to be entirely freaked out. I did share the office. I just didn't notice Neil, whom I shared with, until he popped his head out from behind his computer screen. God was surely channelling Julie Andrews the day he created him. For he is surely the greatest man a dumped girl could wish to share an office with.

I promise that things aren't all going to take a turn for the sitcom at this point. There will be no sitting around drinking coffee with my buddies or staring out of my window typing: 'And then I got to thinking . . .' But for a couple of years I really did live the glorious cliché of sharing an office with the greatest gay workmate a girl could ever ask for. Now, before you get all twitchy about me portraying him as some kind of accessory to be picked up with non-chip nail polish and a Stila lipgloss, I should point out that I didn't realize he was gay for the first four months we shared an office. Yeah, yeah, I know, it's pathetic. The fact that he was less diamanté shirt and plucked eyebrows than the average sitcom would have you believe may have temporarily misled my younger self.

But heaven knows how his love of Jackie Collins or his relentless attempts to integrate 'Fetch!' as a mark of approval into the average Londoner's vocabulary entirely passed me by. Either way, we had become firm friends before his partner – Mark – emailed me an invitation to his thirtieth birthday, and the penny finally dropped. And by that stage it was too late.

What greeted me was not a whirlwind of finger-snapping, lip-pursing and hair-tossing but the biggest, warmest and most heartfelt hug I had ever received. And a bagel on my desk. I cried and cried until I reached the stuttery intake of breath stage, when you can't talk, even if you're starting to feel better.

'I-I-I-I-I-I just don't understand it. What did I do to deserve this?' I managed to blurt out.

'I know, love, I know. There's nothing you've done wrong,' he replied. 'You just can't look at it that way.'

'But we loved each other so much. It was just so right. I was really happy.'

'Were you, though? *Were you*? I mean, you didn't seem that happy when you left the office last night.'

'But I loved him.'

'Did you, though? Really?'

'Yes, of cou-ou-ou-ourse.' Cue more sobs.

'I'm sorry. I know it always hurts. And it's going to hurt for ages. But what I mean is, let's look at this objectively. I know you loved him, or at least you'd got used to loving him, but were you still really in love?'

'Well, *I* was.' Cue sobs getting a little petulant, and possibly some light pouting.

'Yes, yes. I know you *felt* like you still loved him. And rejection stings like an absolute bitch, but let's look at the evidence.'

'But I loved him! And he loved me! I think!' A wail.

'OK, OK. I know. But what I'm trying to say is that, no matter how much you *felt* like you were in love, it just wasn't good enough. He wasn't good enough. For you.'

'What do you mean?' Querulous look from beneath eyes.

'Well, look at some of the things he said to you. I think you are well shot of him.'

'What like?'

'The jaw comment! The jaw comment! Never may the jaw comment go uncommented-upon!'

Ah yes. The Jaw Comment. The perfect example of why Nate and I were never meant to be.

One Saturday morning while we were messing around, listening to the Beach Boys and getting ready to go out for the day, I made the mistake of asking him what he thought was the most beautiful thing about me. This was not *entirely* unprompted, as he had just said that he liked my new coat. I am now fully aware that someone

67

asking such a question in the first place is in a less than ideal relationship. But nothing could have prepared me for the answer. While of course 'Your brilliant tits' might have been a little crude, or 'I've always loved your artistic hands' might have seemed a little too much like struggling to say the right thing, the actual answer – 'I've always found you have a pleasing jaw' – was unforgivable.

Let's be clear about this. It was not a jokey comment. It wasn't a lewd 'Ooh, I bet you can open your mouth really wide' comment. He genuinely meant it. My jaw pleased him more than anything else. I'm not an unreasonable woman: I know it was a tough question to answer. I'm not one for thinking that red roses and country walks are all it takes to be romantic. But you've almost got to admire his commitment to a total *lack* of romance. Honestly, it must actually require quite a lot of imagination to come up with something as unutterably without charm as 'I've always found you have a pleasing jaw'. It's like someone named Giuseppe Montebravo asking what you most love about Rome, and replying, 'Oh, I've always found the municipal bus links terribly efficient.'

Neil looked at me expectantly. 'A pleasing jaw?!' he yelped. 'Judd Nelson in *The Breakfast Club* has a pleasing jaw. Come on, you *know* you can do better than him!'

I sighed, limply conceding that The Jaw Comment was indeed not a moment to cherish. But here's the rub.

When you've just been freshly dumped, nothing and no one can convince your bludgeoned heart that the things he did wrong weren't somehow solvable, if only you were given the chance to try a little harder. Your heart and your head are two walkers taking a hike on a sunny day, but each with radically different approaches. My head was the sensible walker – armed with a comprehensive map, a broad-rimmed hat, a stout pair of boots, and a bottle of water. Perhaps it was even wearing a pair of khaki shorts. It knew the road ahead was tough, but it understood how to get there and was adequately equipped for the journey: less than twenty-four hours after the demise of Me + Nate, my head could quite clearly comprehend that there were many flaws in our relationship, and that it was probably best that someone had finally called time on it. My heart, however, was behaving shamefully. You see, it hadn't had proper notice, so it wasn't up for the hike at all. Decked out in a pair of fetching but impractical sparkly flip-flops, a strappy top which was already starting to rub, and carrying nothing but a sticky ice cream for nourishment, it was already deeply unhappy about the road ahead. The heat was bearing down, and the misery was setting in.

So there was I, stuck in the middle, with common sense blaring in one ear, while the other was filled with ghastly needy drivel such as: 'If he'd just call me, then he would be able to tell just from the tone of my voice that I will change whatever needs to be changed and then we can go back to being blissfully happy and in love. Really quickly.' Shameful, shameful thoughts! But so easy to think ... You see, that's the trouble with being dumped – you haven't prepared yourself for it. If you had prepared yourself for it, and you really wanted it, then it would simply be that mythical beast The Amicable Split. These are as common as unicorns. *Someone* always decides – and rarely when the other is expecting it. When it isn't you doing the deciding, you're d.u.m.p.e.d. Even if things were rocky when the break-up happened, it still doesn't feel like your choice. You didn't get to do the spurning, because you still had hope, or maybe even a little confidence. When that's whipped away from you, you feel the sting.

Neil's eyes were starting to dart from side to side rather worryingly, betraying the fact that he was fast running out of inspiring bons mots. Then he was, quite literally, saved by the bell. Well, not strictly a bell, but the telephone on my desk ringing. I slightly forgot that I was at work and leaped on it, eager for a new set of ears to hear my plight. Instead, my ears were assaulted by Cecilia Bartoli singing her heart out, accompanied by shrill bird-song. In what seemed like the very far distance was a woman's voice, yelping, 'How dare he! How dare he!'

It was my mother. And her canary. Let me explain.

My father worked abroad, and my parents were moving from an army quarter to a new apartment near to the barracks where he would soon be working. As the new barracks were in Italy, there were complications with the move (the apartment was currently bright yellow, which my mother was refusing to live with). While the apartment was being painted my parents had been put in a small local hotel. They hadn't told the hotelier that Monty, my mother's canary, was staying too. He and his cage had been smuggled in under a bundle of coats and my parents had committed themselves to playing ear-bleedingly loud music whenever the canary was awake in order to cover up the telltale singing.

My father had bought Monty as a gift for my mother in Brussels' Grand Place bird market when my brother, the youngest sibling, left home. I think my father thought he would provide an amusing diversion for a few months until he flew out into the garden to be eaten by a cat, or my mother got bored and gave him to a neighbour's daughter. Instead, Monty proved the ultimate antidote to empty nest syndrome and my mother adored that bird with a passion even Long John Silver would have marvelled at. He went on to defy all of the statistics on the many, many online canary message boards that my mother frequented. (There is a website for 'avian attire' that she will tell you about if you ask her nicely.)

For a start, there was the trilling. Though the breed is not meant to be a songbird, that scrap of fluff was singing constantly. When I say sing I mean relentless birdsong. If it wasn't actual song then it was curious repetitive beeps like a fax machine. Then, after months of closing all the windows on stiflingly hot days – and much encouragement with trails of endive left in eye-catching locations throughout the house – my mother trained him to leave his cage. Eventually, she could just put her finger into the cage, and he'd hop onto it like Mary Poppins with the robin feathering his nest. The pièce de résistance came after a summer of my mother wearing a lettuce leaf on her head, which finally led to Monty flying out of his cage to perch directly on her while she wandered around the house getting along with life's daily chores. It was in this position that I imagined them when my mother called that morning.

'How dare he!' my mother continued.

'Mum, is that you? How are you?'

'I'm fine. Lily called me – she's told me the whole saga. I'm so sorry. It's a bloody outrage the way he's treated you. You must feel awful. It just hurts and hurts, doesn't it?' My mother is, shall we say, a little 'Latin' of temperament. Never one to grasp an understatement with warm, welcoming arms, she is always keen to express her feelings flamboyantly. She's empathetic to the point where

I've sometimes wondered if she just sees emoting as a hobby. My father on the other hand prefers maps and list-making.

Being the product of two such different personalities has often made Lily and me a little confusing for our boyfriends. One moment we're scouring atlases for the most time-efficient route to a party, and the next we're windmilling our arms and raising our eyebrows, trying to make ourselves understood on a very important (but probably rather small) point.

'I just feel so stupid, Mum. Why didn't I see it coming? Why didn't anyone see it coming? It all feels so sudden.'

'Oh, darling, we all saw it coming. He wore far too much brown and he wasn't good enough for you anyway.'

'But Mum, you'll never believe anyone is good enough for me or Lily.' Then I realized what she'd said first. 'He wore too much brown?'

'Yes, it was so depressing. It was dampening your spirits, I could tell. Obviously no one is going to be good enough for you in my eyes, but he was so dour.'

'You're so right. He's probably evil and wearing brown because it's some kind of cult uniform.' I was starting to get into the swing of it now. Irrationality always seemed to work for her.

'Exactly. And he gave you those stupid mittens for

Christmas when Lily got a Gucci wallet from Jake. I know you said it was a really lovely gift as they were knitted by women in Afghanistan, but I saw your face when you both opened your presents at the same time.'

I don't want to dwell on that Christmas. Nate believed he was being thoughtful when he bought me those mittens. People *do* get cold hands in winter. But unfortunately, just as I started to get into the swing of hating him, I realized that it wasn't at all comforting. Simply thinking about how he had tried to get me a great present, only to get it so tragically wrong, set me off again. I started sobbing.

'Don't worry, they were only mittens. There will be other Christmases – and other boyfriends! Thank God!' screamed my mum over some of Monty's finer fax-esque trills.

'It's not that,' I explained through the mist of fresh tears. 'It's just that now I realize how it wasn't working, I feel like such an idiot for loving him so much. We had so much fun together; we were a real team sometimes. He did loads of lovely things for me that I forgot to tell people. I really, really miss him so much that it feels like a physical pain. If he was so bloody awful that everyone saw it coming and thought I should have got there first, what kind of an idiot does that make me? Now, on top of missing him *and* feeling totally wretched that I have been dumped again, I have to feel completely ashamed of being such a dunce for falling in love with him in the first place.'

'Oh, darling, none of that's your fault. If we could control whom we fell in love with then falling in love wouldn't be so deliriously exciting. All of those inexplicable excitements would mean nothing if it was a rational decision.'

'Great, now you're getting all romantic on me.'

'It's not that – I'm simply trying to explain that we can't help who we fall for, no matter how ghastly they may be.'

I couldn't help thinking that no matter how comforting my mother was trying to be, her comments, combined with what Jo had told me the night before, weren't much help. In fact, it was all making me feel like more of an idiot, giving me the distinct impression certain people had just been tolerating Nate for my sake.

By the time I'd finished talking to my mum, Neil had left the office for a meeting, and I realized it was time to collect Larry Hagman for his day's interviews. It wasn't nearly as exhausting as I had dreaded, and I was actually glad of the distraction. By four o'clock I had kept my bottom lip under control for almost the whole day and was looking forward to the last interview. I had arranged for him to meet the journalist in one of my favourite cafés in the centre of town. Once again my mind had been playing evil tricks, because as we pulled up to the patis-serie I remembered that it was where Nate and I had spent one of our first dates. As we walked into the café and I introduced the journalist to the Lovely Larry I was sud-denly overwhelmed by a huge wave of longing for Nate. I wouldn't be able to call him at the end of the day and tell him proudly how well it had gone with an important client, and hear his praise and encouragement. More cru-cially, I realized how much these places meant to me. The venues for our first dates were a slice of our history – key parts of the Legend of Us that existed in my head (and, clearly, mine alone). Instead of being lovely cafés or bars or parks, they were miserable reminders. They were no longer cathedrals to romance, but monuments to my broken heart. I was going to have to reclaim most of my favourite areas of the city where I lived so that I could learn to love them again for them, instead of for the treasured memories that they held for me.

As the journalist left and Larry went to buy a box of fancy chocolates for his wife, I started to see the enormity of the task ahead of me. By the time we got into the awaiting Daimler, two huge tears plopped onto the folder I was holding on my lap. But no gulpy sobs this time, you'll be pleased to know. Larry turned to ask me if I was all right. Unable to contain myself after a day of such extreme professionalism and proficiently self-contained expertise, I burst into tears. 'I'm terribly sorry! I shouldn't be telling you this, but I'm just really upset because I broke up with my boyfriend yesterday.'

'Oh my gaaaaaad, your puuuur thang! Whadda gaaaa go 'n' do a thing laaaak that to a purdy gurl laaaak yew fur?'

I was getting used to his accent by now, so I didn't need to double take. 'I don't know, I really don't. I suppose it's for the best. I'm so sorry for crying, though.'

'Don't yew wuurry about a thang, mah deeer.'

The car continued in silence for the rest of the short journey back to Larry's swanky hotel on Piccadilly. As it pulled up he shuffled around in his bag for a minute, wrote down some notes and then prepared to get out. The driver came around and opened Larry's door, skilfully avoiding eye contact with what he very obviously considered to be the Crazy Weeping Publicist. But before he got out, Larry thrust a couple of things into my hands. 'Wuhn's to cheer yew up 'cuz ah know gurrls lahk it, and wuhn's cuz I know yew know Laaaah-tn.'

Once the driver, now visibly on edge at being left alone in the car with me, started the car to drop me back at the office, I looked down at what had been left in my lap. It was the box of chocolates that Larry had just bought for his wife, and a copy of his autobiography. On the title page was written: 'To Dear Alex, *Nil Illigitimus Carbarundum*'.

'Well, what the hell does that mean, you nerd?' was Lily's response when I told her my touching story before leaving work.

'Don't let the bastards get you down! Isn't that sweet?' I replied.

'I suppose so. But it's a bit weird that J.R. was nice to you in Latin. How are you otherwise?'

'Oh, just a total wreck. I have a terrible hangover, and no food at home. And my flatmates are out so I think I'm going to spend the night at home crying.'

Lily has always been very specific with me about how to deal with certain situations, and the first twenty-four hours of a break-up turned out to be one of them. 'Now Ali,' she began, 'you are talking bullshit. You need to treat this as war. You versus your heartache. And it will NOT defeat you. No, Ali, I won't let it. And nor will you.'

'Um. OK. Why have you gone all military? It's kind of scary.'

'Don't try to undermine me with cheek. I will come round this evening with a copy of *Dirty Dancing*. But only on one condition.'

'Do I have to do press-ups? Cos I'm really feeling kind of weak.'

'Nothing you will go through will be as bad as this first twenty-four hours. You feel like Martin Sheen going mad in front of the hotel-room mirror in *Apocalypse Now*. Ha haaa, you probably even look like Martin Sheen going mad in front of the hotel-room mirror in *Apocalypse Now!*' She chuckled to herself a little more, noticeably more amused by this analogy than I was. I sighed. 'I will come round this evening as long as you listen to my rules, and you write them down. Because you must study and understand your enemy to be its victor.'

'Seriously. You sound like Russell Crowe in *Gladiator*. If you turn up wearing those sandals you bought with me last summer . . .'

'Concentrate! This is a battle you will win. So don't panic, listen to my rules, and take notes.'

4

The First Twenty-Four Hours (of War): Lily's Battle Tactics

As ever, it turned out that Lily was pretty much right. Her advice on how to get through the first twenty-four hours proved invaluable – if slightly late this time. She wasn't joking when she said that getting over heartache was a battle. It's war: not you versus him, but you versus your hurt. A relationship and its recovery are like a bullet and its wound: the bullet slips in so quickly and smoothly that you barely even notice it happening, but getting it out is hideous, agonizing and causes scarring. But it can be conquered. Why do you think Action Man had a scar anyway? Because they're cool. So, approach that first day like war, and you may find yourself stronger than you ever imagined you could be.

Camouflage

There is a lot to be said for the simple act of not giving up entirely on how you look. It may even help to employ some faux military accessorizing. I'm not talking strictly Doctor Martens and mud-stained cheeks, but some martial buttons would do to help you get in the mood and remind yourself what you're up against. Perhaps a charm bracelet with a small pistol? Perhaps not.

You just need to find a combination of style and practicality that works for you. Maybe you can't be bothered to put on a full face of make-up, but you absolutely cannot give in completely. Wearing heels can make you feel like you're still a lady in charge of her destiny, and then there are the myriad hair products and styling opportunities you could treat yourself to. No one has ever been known to feel worse after a blow-dry. Lily claims to be particularly fond of the idea of wearing your most glamorous and sexy underwear, safe in the knowledge that you are doing it to please no one but yourself. In extreme cases, wear no knickers, as suggested to me by my grandmother, the minxy old dear.

A Secure Base Camp

In the battle for survival it is of paramount importance to get home and create a safe area for retreat. You've all seen *Lost*. You know how they love to make stuff cosy in the jungle. I'm talking about making your bedroom feel like a sanctuary, rather than just a room with half as many people in it as usual.

Wash your sheets. This is essential. Not because you are a messy little slut who needs a kick up the arse to get your life in order, but because human smell is so extraordinarily evocative – if he's been in your bed recently, you'll be able to tell. So, the best thing to do is to wash and change your sheets as soon as possible, with a totally random soap powder. This will help to minimise the suffering in case you wake up in the middle of the night to find yourself fighting crushing grief when all the fun people are asleep and there's nothing good on telly. In the event that this happens, you don't want smell to trick you into being reminded of him. The sudden sensation of having no one on hand to touch is a truly comprehensive kick in the guts – but I'm afraid the only solution is to howl like a baby until your eyes are so red that you can't not fall back to sleep.

But remember, if you have set up a fabulously

secure base camp then you've always got somewhere to hide for those goddamn awful moments before you're ready to start high-kicking your way back to life.

Note: you have gone too far if you are using sand-bags for scatter cushions.

Lines of Communication

Many a war has been won or lost on account of the quality of communication amongst the troops. This is an elaborate way for me to try and make you feel like a powerful Buffy-type warrior while I tell you to make sure you DON'T CALL HIM.

I am begging you, please. No, in fact I am ordering you in a bellowing sergeant-major voice. Do. Not. Call. Him. No good can come of it.

We've all heard that insistent first-24-hours voice squeaking away at the back of our minds: 'What if I call him now, surely he'll understand what a massive mis-take he's made?'; 'What if I call him now and he realizes the enormous bond between us which of course means he'll immediately want me back?'; 'What if he's broken up with his new boyfriend-stealing harpy and remem-bered *I'm* brilliant and clearly the best girlfriend ever?'; 'What if I ring him, and I don't even speak, but when he sees my number on his phone it'll remind him of all the good times we had together and then everything'll be fine again?'

We've all been there, and that voice is a cohort of the enemy! It is an evil spy sent specifically to confuse you and make you get up to no good. That voice is the very Mata Hari of heartache, luring you towards mayhem with false pledges and promises of a good time if you do things her way. SHE MUST BE RESISTED. The truth is that ringing him straightaway to plead your case isn't going to get anybody anywhere. If you're going to get back together and he's on the way to concluding he's made a horrible mistake, then it can wait a day or two until you're both feeling a little more rational. But the harsh truth is that in most cases, you're not going to get back together, and this is a good thing, so you need to just summon all of your energy and confidence and hug it towards you instead of him, because you need it and you deserve it.

Remember, girls, you don't want the indignity of being dumped and then doing or saying something shaming immediately afterwards. This is shoddy military behaviour and no one, not even Private Benjamin, would condone it. There are very few girls (or indeed boys) who've never checked their recently dialled numbers only to realize that they've made a drunken amorous call but have no idea what they said. Sure, if you're actually in a relationship you can get away with that – OK, so the leery voice might not be brilliant but if the intentions are good, those calls are usually received in good grace. But post-dumping calls are the dark, evil twin of drunken booty calls – rarely received favourably and unlikely to achieve anything positive.

So, and I know you're not going to like this: DELETE HIS NUMBERS. Yes, I really really mean it. Friends will have his number if there is an emergency that does require you to contact him. Even if you don't intend to call him screaming and shouting with anger and vitriol, it simply won't do to be making 'I was just calling to make sure you got home OK' calls, or texting 'Sleep well and thanks for everything' before you go to bed. Your motives will be utterly transparent. You are without doubt going to cope just as well if you don't make these little gestures towards conciliatory com-munication. Even better, in fact, because that way you can't possibly spend the next two days analysing his response, or absence of it.

Now listen up. I know this is going to sound tough, but at this stage I would also suggest that you delete your emails to and from him, along with his email address. While they are undeniably convenient, emails can actually be poison to relationships. You have too much time to try and compose an utterly unrealistic 'best' version of yourself and your arguments, and there is far too much space for misinterpretation, particularly at this delicate stage.

Lines of communication effectively sorted, battle is always easier.

Allies

A warrior is nothing without trusted allies. Finding allies isn't that tricky, but knowing which ones are to be trusted is harder. But that doesn't mean you should reject all unknowns. Some people whom you may have only recently got to know during the course of this latest relationship might reveal themselves to be far fonder of you than you imagined. I have gone for months, or even years, thinking that someone was a little snooty or aloof (or, to be honest, just prettier and cleverer than me and therefore intimidating), only to find out later that they're merely rather shy people who reserve expressions of affection or emotion for particular moments. This is one of the unexpected bonuses of your predicament – Break-up Buddies! Scoop them all up like a kid nicking sweets from Woolworths – you're going to need them, and, more importantly, you're going to have lots of fun with them in the coming months.

However, if your relationship had been making you unhappy for a little while before the end, or if it was one that you embarked upon against the advice of any friends or family, there may well be a couple of 'I told you so's. These will sting like hell. It will be hard, but try to ignore them. Rise above them. Anyone who dares to say 'I told you so' to a girl who has been freshly dumped should be forced to parade up and down Oxford Street with an enormous sign on their back saying: 'My Friend Went Out With Someone Unsuitable And Then When He Dumped Her I Was A Bit Sanctimonious About It.' (I told you it was a big sign.)

But you get my point: if anyone's going to treat you like that then you mustn't take it personally; instead you should stand up straight, safe in the knowledge that they were probably trying to do the right thing, and feel relieved to have seen this side to them now rather than later. And then spend a little more time with some of your more sympathetic or more fun friends.

During a war against heartbreak a golden rule is: Be Nice to His Friends. Ringing them up the day you get dumped in order to bitch about him isn't wise, but his mates can come in handy offering a huge amount of comfort. Indeed, I have made many good friends out of the friends of exes. They are, in human terms, the *Blockbusters* dictionary of relationships: you failed and didn't get to come home with the prize (which was admittedly only an eighties computer game or a heavily supervised trip to Stratford-upon-Avon anyway), but in years to come any contestant would surely treasure their signed Blockbusters dictionary far above and beyond any fond memories they may have had for an actual prize. In these first tender twenty-four hours you might feel as if you've lost the prize, but in fact you can come away with something that will ultimately give you more joy and much more support.

In case I haven't made myself clear enough (am standing in full military regalia now – with baton!), even if you feel like ringing up everyone he ever met to tell them how much you hate him, just don't.

Diversionary Tactics

The enemy is heartbreak, and the successful warrior needs to be prepared for it to pounce at any minute. She needs to try and find ways to keep it otherwise occupied.

During these first twenty-four hours, your mind is racing like a gazelle, randomly pouncing on forgotten facts and memories just as you try to get anything done. As you stand at the kettle trying to make that eighteenth cup of tea you find yourself suddenly shrieking, 'I can't believe I went to all that bloody effort to try and cook his parents Sunday lunch that time!' or, 'Oh, bollocks, I've left my favourite nail polish under his bedside table. How the hell am I going to get that back now?'

This is not a good time to try and watch something that involves a coherent narrative. The whole 'let's sit down and watch *Bridget Jones* – she's crap too' mentality, or even 'let's watch something romantic to give us hope' quite frankly doesn't make sense. Maybe in a couple of weeks you'll be up to it, but for now, you simply don't have the attention span to deal with a plot. However, anything that isn't immediately exciting or interesting will give your sorrowful little mind time to drift into misery.

What you really need to be watching is a selection of trash which can make you laugh and bitch about people. The E! Channel is ideal – the heartache, the drugs, the painful plastic surgery disasters. All will improve your outlook dramatically.

Covert Operations

Aka somewhere undercover to cry. Everyone needs a back-up plan for when field operations get too risky. In the first twenty-four hours after being dumped, randomly bursting into tears is an unavoidable part of your life. This is as it should be. Crying is indescribably cathartic, allowing you to surrender to your heartache while providing an excellent and effective way to get attention from friends who will then offer you sympathy, and possibly some chocolate. Trying to keep a lid on a simmering cauldron of tears can become intolerably exhausting for even the mightiest warrior after a few hours.

So give in for fifteen minutes every now and again. Go on, actually *try* to make yourself cry as much as possible for a little bit every few hours. Because it's the only thing harder than trying not to cry. Those tears will just sit inside you if you don't get them out – so go for it now, rather than freaking yourself out later.

It's not such a great idea to do it in public though – perhaps this is something you can only get away with once. Make sure you are in a safe place or at least with people you know for the first day or so. If you live alone, make sure there's someone who knows where you are, and if you don't live alone, make sure someone's home. If you lived with him, then go and stay with an understanding friend. There's only so much public sobbing anyone can do.

Likewise, although no one wants to embarrass themselves at work or at college, there's usually at least one person you can tell who has a nice office you can hide in if you feel wobbly the next day. Find them.

Rations

An army marches on its stomach. This is well known. What is less well known is that it's highly likely that this brigade against heartache will also be marching on a substantial amount of alcohol. This in turn means that you need adequate rations to sustain you. We're all familiar with that peculiar, tight feeling in the stomach – when you're least expecting it you feel starving, but confronted with the idea of actual food you immediately feel overwhelmed and unable to eat anything at all. This feeling is swiftly interchangeable with an insatiable desire to eat shameful amounts of comfort food. And then there are the after-effects of the copious sympathy drinks you will be bought, and the countless cups of tea or coffee you'll be drinking. Stock up on goodies, but make sure you buy some juice and some vitamins too. No one wants to admit that their ex hurt them so much they developed scurvy.

Whatever you do during this first day, don't ever forget that things will get better. It's unrealistic to put a timescale on things, but soon you'll start to feel normal, and after a while you'll start to have fun, and then a few months later you'll wake up one morning smiling, yet waiting for the kick in the guts to hit you, and it won't come. You'll stop thinking of him as an actual person. He'll be less of a human being, more of an era, like the Renaissance or the Industrial Revolution. One day soon, if you see him in person, it will be more like looking at a photograph of yourself as a child in the seventies – you'll know you were there, you'll think it looked like it was OK, but you won't really be able to remember it or believe that it actually happened to you. Because you're happy again.

5

The Rebound

There was still one nagging thought at the back of my mind. I needed to get some of my belongings from Nate's house: my spare toothbrush, a cookery book and some treasured cosmetics, for starters. After a few months of going out with him, I'd been allocated a small area on his bookcase for some of my necessary 'staying over' items, and – mindful not to freak him out with overtures towards Actually Moving In – I had carefully decanted small amounts of moisturiser, foundation etc. into tiny sample bottles. Admittedly, I didn't strictly *need* them back now. But I am not a wasteful person, and I kept thinking that if they weren't needed at Nate's house any more, those tiny bottles would be really useful for taking to the gym. And if I went to collect them from him in person, he would almost definitely see me, realize he had made a horrible mistake, and beg me to come back. Plus, that Jamie Oliver book was clearly a classic in the making and I really wanted to keep what I now thought was probably a first edition. And if I went to collect it from him in person, he would almost definitely see me, realize he had made a horrible mistake, and beg me to come back. Further to that, I am a terribly environmentally conscious person, so of course the idea of just throwing away a toothbrush that had been used a mere couple of times a week for only a few months was abhorrent to me. The waste of plastic would be unforgivable! And if I went to collect it from him in person, he would almost definitely see me, realize he had made a horrible mistake, and beg me to come back. So, when I mentioned to Jo and Lily that at the weekend I should probably pop over and collect a couple of things from Nate's, I was met with a military movement of hands onto hips and a collective bellowing of, 'NO. *I'll* go!' But I was determined that it was me who should do it; to go and collect my belongings myself would provide me with a healthy moment of closure. And if I went to collect them from him in person, he would almost definitely see me, realize he had made a horrible mistake, and beg me to come back. I put forward a convincing argument, but it wasn't convincing enough for those two.

'We know why you want to go. It's just to get all maudlin looking at the rooms where you had such a good time,' suggested Lily.

'And so that you can get into one of your long and tortured heart-to-hearts with him, so you can try and persuade him of things he doesn't really believe. And he'll pretend to agree with you because he'll be feeling guilty,' added Jo.

'But it'll only make you feel worse. They're only rooms. Swizzle round! Look forward and start thinking about new places for good times.'

'Surely you know that even if he *did* love you with all his heart, it just wasn't working out?'

Yeah, yeah, YEAH. I knew all of these things. But I wanted that moment. Admittedly I was starting to have the first inkling that perhaps Nate and I hadn't had the kind of relationship that was going to either last or make me happy in the long run, but I was still smarting from having all the power of deciding when to bail out taken from me. I wanted my end-of-a-chick-flick moment. I wanted to be Reese Witherspoon or Sandra Bullock saying my piece for what was right and good. I wanted to let him know that I was going to be Just Fine without him, as the music swelled in my head.

At no point was there any part of me thinking that if I went to see him in person, he would almost definitely see me, realize he had made a horrible mistake, and beg me to come back.

'What music?' asked Lily. 'Now you've got me really worried.'

101

'You know what I mean. The inspiring music that heralds the moment when I seize back a smidgen of self-respect.'

'It's a very high-risk strategy. Do you really think it'll make you feel better? Let me go for you. I'll be fair and not get involved,' promised Jo, only slightly insincerely.

'No, I want to prove to myself that I can do this. I really think it would help.'

Eventually it was agreed that I would be allowed to go and collect my belongings, but definitely not until the weekend, by which time I was to have undertaken an extensive programme of further rehabilitation activities.

That night Nate's friend James came over to my house in what had become his official position as Ambassador for Nate's Friends. He didn't wear formal regalia, but he did convey the message loud and clear that I was not being dumped by Nate's mates. They all still loved me and wanted to keep in touch with me, James in particular. He feigned disloyalty to Nate for my sake and obligingly said lots of what I wanted to hear: Nate was an idiot, he'd never find anyone like me, he didn't know what he was doing, they would all miss seeing less of me. In retrospect, perhaps he didn't say 'idiot', but it felt like it and that's what counted.

During the days at the office Neil continued to make

sure that I was well stocked with bagels and that I didn't miss any crucial meetings. Larry Hagman was dispatched back to the States, his tour now over. The next night I went to the gym with Sally and her sister, except we didn't do much exercise. I just went on a guest pass to their fancy, bleached-pine gym and we did a few leisurely lengths in the swimming pool before spending ages in the steam room and sauna, gossiping and sweating off some of the alcohol and caffeine from the last few days.

And then it was the weekend. I had written the necessary stiffly formal emails arranging to go to Nate's house on the Saturday morning, thus giving me the entire weekend to recover from any potential dignity-related issues. Despite it being a drizzly November day, I rummaged around in my drawers and found my biggest pair of sunglasses. I mentally prepared my speech, and set off for south London. It was all going to be fine.

Except that the bus took quite a long time to arrive, and then there was quite a lot of traffic. So by the time I arrived at his house, I was a strange combination of incredibly bored and feverishly stressed. My body was slightly clammy with sweat and rain, I really needed to pee and I'd been through my chick-flick speech so many times in my head that I was starting to forget it. I rang the bell with trepidation. Nate answered it a moment later. He looked exactly the same. No horns, no menacing grimace. He looked just like him. Of course he did, but it just seemed so unexpected. Now that he'd been categorized differently in my mind, and now that I was having to make such huge changes because of him, I'd somehow thought he'd have an entirely new wardrobe or something.

'Hi.'

'Hi.' I pushed my large sunglasses up off my face and onto my head. They promptly slammed down again, landing somewhere near my chin.

'Um, come in.'

'Thanks. Can I use your bathroom?'

'Of course. You know where it is.'

Indeed I did. I locked myself in, took the sunglasses off completely and leaned against the door for a minute. I breathed in, I breathed out. I tried to remember my speech and couldn't. Then I went to the loo. At least I went at the right moment this time – I was getting better already.

When I walked back into his living room I noticed that Nate had packed my belongings up into a cardboard box and immediately felt a lump in my throat. I was amazed at how much stuff there was.

'I just wanted to say . . .' he began. I felt sick. 'That I'm sorry it didn't work out.'

Hmph, I thought. If you're so frickin' sorry then why did you end it?

'I think you're an amazing, amazing person . . .'

Hang on a minute. This isn't supposed to happen. Don't say decent things. You're evil.

'. . . and I really want us to stay friends.'

'*Friends?!*' I regained my composure and did a majestic harrumph. Fragments of the speech were starting to come back to me. 'FRIENDS? If there's one thing I've learned this week it's that I don't want for friends. Since you dropped your little bombshell I have truly understood what it means to be a friend. It doesn't mean an awkward drink with someone every three months, just so that when you see them in the street one day when you're out with your next girlfriend you needn't feel a cold shiver of fear in case they go up and tell her that you dump people when the going gets tough. Nor does it mean including someone on funny group emails forwarding wry jokes about Al Gore or screen grabs from Big Brother just so that you can get a sound night's sleep while they're sobbing into their pillow, wondering why you didn't give them a chance to try and work things out. No, "friends" are people who put themselves out to make sure that others are OK. They don't mind when people are a little irrational because they're hurt or insecure. They don't turn off their phone when people they care about are walking home alone. And none of them have ever noticed what kind of a jaw I have. So you can keep your friendship and shove it up your arse. Now I'll take my stuff and be out of your hair, thank you very much, *mate*.'

I did it! I actually did it. I said my speech without crying, stumbling or accidentally inserting the wrong terminology at a crucial point. And what's more, as the imaginary soundtrack started to play in my head, I managed to pick up my box of belongings and leave the house with dignity. I didn't look back once. I walked up the hill from his house and sat down at the bus stop, feeling numb. I knew what I'd said was true, but what's more, it dawned on me that I didn't really want him now. While of course I still wanted to be wanted by him, I could see that it was never going to work out. I was clearly getting very good at break-ups.

I was beginning to pat myself on the back for my courage under fire when I heard someone shouting my name. I looked up, and saw it was Nate. He was running at me full pelt, absolutely shrieking my name. I then noticed that my bus was coming up behind him. He saw it too, and started to run even faster to the point where his arms had gone all waggly and weird – he was trying to get to me before the bus! This was it. The dream! He had realized the error of his ways and was coming to beg me to come back. I couldn't believe it. I immediately threw all thoughts of dignity and survival aside (along with my cardboard box) and leaped up. 'Yes! Yes!' I called back.

The bus slowed towards the stop as I turned my back on it to face Nate, who had reached me. And just as I did, I worked out what was happening. He had my sunglasses in his hand. 'You left them in the bathroom,' he said, and handed them over as the bus I'd ignored pulled away again. He smiled bleakly, registering what I must have thought.

'Thank you,' I mumbled.

Somewhat apologetically, he turned and walked slowly back down the hill. He didn't look around once. I hobbled back to the bus stop, sat down and sobbed. It didn't matter that I was realizing the relationship wasn't working: I still had no taste for rejection. And now it felt like I'd been rejected twice. It really, really hurt. This was going to take a little longer than I'd hoped.

I was lucky enough that evening to have a fresh perspective on my break-up. A male perspective. How wonderful, how balanced and healing, I hear you think. Hmmm. Sally had dragged me out to a party, not wanting me to develop scary hermit-like tendencies. Unfortunately it was a really busy party – the kind where there's almost nowhere to stand without being in the way of someone slightly drunker than you. And no matter how much I drank, everyone seemed to be slightly drunker than me. I was just getting tired, leaden limbs and droopy eyelids, while everyone else was starting to whoop with joy, throwing their heads back ever further as they laughed and celebrated the very wonder of being alive and in love that night.

The only person who didn't seem to be joining in this bacchanalian frenzy was Sally's boyfriend Pete. He was a little curmudgeonly at the best of times, in a good, avuncular kind of way, but this was a party where he hardly knew anyone, so he seemed pretty happy to perch in a corner with me. He was trying hard to be empathetic to my plight, but was woefully ill-equipped. When Sally had told me once that he knew lots about the birds and the bees, I'd thought she was being uncharacteristically raunchy, and I felt a little awkward. But it turned out that Pete really did know lots about actual birds and actual bees. He's a bookish sort. I realized the extent of his inadequacies regarding my fragile state when I started to babble nervously at him, becoming ever more frustrated and overwhelmed by the number of people who were asking after Nate, and where he was. Pete sympathetically patted me on the shoulder and said, 'Of course, if you really think about it, all getting over someone involves is reformatting some basic behavioural patterns.'

Oh, OF COURSE, I thought to myself. Silly me, why didn't I get to grips with that earlier? I hadn't realized that all it entailed was basic reformatting. Is that all? So, just to clarify, it's merely a question of changing the way I feel about EVERYTHING I'VE EVER CARED ABOUT. Forgive me if I'm being pernickety about nailing it down, but are you really saying that it's only a simple case of ENTIRELY REFOCUSING my emotions, the very core of my being and that which encourages me to get up in the morning? It's just that it seems like such an unbelievably good bargain to TOTALLY REWIRE YOUR HEART in exchange for being over someone. Well, there we have it, the deal of the century! And who'd have thought it was so quick and easy. I'll sort that out as I walk back to the tube, shall I? SHALL I? Or perhaps I'll travel home on my unicycle, just to make things a little more challenging for myself.'

I smiled weakly at Pete and said I was going to head home. I trudged back to the tube alone, remembering the special look that Nate and I used to give each other when we were ready to leave a party.

'Oh, come on, Ali, it's not *that* bad,' suggested Lily when I called her after midnight, finally home, alone and by now in tears again. 'You know what Pete actually meant. It's unavoidable that you'll start to feel better. After all, what else are you going to do? Die of a broken heart? Ha haa! You're already doing so well – look at this morning! Don't keep trying so hard to get over him; you're exhausting yourself and it's barely been a week. Just concentrate on making yourself a bit happier, and forget about making it all about him and getting over him. You can't force it. Anyway, in my opinion, you only really get over someone once you're in love with someone else.'

And only a couple of weeks later that someone else came along . . .

Scott was a friend of a friend who I'd met a few times while I was with Nate, but I'd always been so busy trying to please Nate I'd never quite noticed him properly. He'd heard I was single, got hold of my email (pretending he wanted some work advice) and before I realized what was happening we were having a drink together. It was all rather intoxicating. When I turned up at the pub he was carrying a copy of Nabokov's *Pale Fire* and drinking a pint of Guinness. I suspected immediately that he fancied me, and was thrilled – not because I fancied him especially but because it was the first time someone clearly cooler than me had shown any interest. But not only was he cool, he was charming. He was everything Nate wasn't: he had an asymmetrical haircut, wore T-shirts with hip logos and was a singer in a band. He worked in TV and knew stuff about MTV presenters and backstage gossip about pop stars. He went on exciting-sounding work trips to New York which he told me about while I embroidered elaborate fantasies about our first trip there together. And he said he liked my trousers.

Just hanging around with Scott made me feel a thousand times better about myself than I had done for months. Instead of feeling the pressure to be a 'good' girlfriend I was free to just concentrate on being fun, funny and sexy. I had spent an awful lot of time recently trying to be agreeable, somehow trying to earn love in a way that is uniquely exhausting and only really possible in a relationship that's on its last legs. But Scott didn't seem very interested in my cooking a pleasing casserole on a Sunday night, or my ability to be polite to parents at Christmas time. He looked at me in a weird, slightly dirty sideways look that you normally only see men doing in aftershave adverts. And he didn't try to hide it at all. He was very nonchalant about his knowledge of all the cool bands and indeed brands. Of course, I'm now sure it was all somewhat studied, but he was so breezy about the way he dropped names that I just breezed along with it, convincing myself I was part of his giddy world. I was desired, not tolerated.

As far as I was concerned, I wasn't going to have

to follow Pete's alarmingly simplistic advice at all – no reformatting of behavioural patterns required! I could just swap and carry on as before. Quite frankly, who needs all that tiresome 'I'm just going to spend some time taking care of myself and thinking about what I really want out of life' phase when you're lucky enough to find someone else who's so lovely immediately after a painful break-up? And what a coincidence that he's the Anti-Nate! Isn't it funny how life works out?

Well, that's what I spent the next couple of months thinking. My friends were good enough to go along with it. None of them went as far as to point out that it was perfectly obvious the whole enterprise was doomed. Jo was polite to him when he came over, and no one else really met him. My mum certainly never heard about him, and Lily had a detached sense of intrigue about him, perhaps suspecting that I wasn't going to talk about this one too much. Apart from Jo, I never introduced him to any of my friends, and he never introduced me to any of his. Perhaps this should have been the first clue that it wasn't going to go anywhere. In fact, he didn't seem to have that many proper friends at all. He told me he had no friends from his childhood, which perhaps should have made me a little bit suspicious about his attitude towards commitment. I suppose I just wasn't that interested in his friends. We spent a lot of time in the pub located between my house and his, a lot of time in his bedroom watching TV. And, um, some other stuff. To be honest, it was mostly the other stuff. There *was* a lot of that. It cheered me up enormously to feel this sexy and desirable. But it's so clear now: in retrospect, I was sexy and desirable at the expense of almost everything else about myself. This began to show on our one trip outside of our postcode, when we went to the Tate Modern – it became increasingly clear that we had absolutely nothing to say to each other. At the time, we just pretended we were being quiet because we were looking at the art. I don't think either of us believed it.

But none of that mattered, because the whole experience was so intoxicating! It was beyond exhilarating to find that someone other than Nate was prepared to be with me. I didn't have to go to bed alone and sob into my pillow – in fact, I stopped crying altogether. And all of the extra time I'd had on my hands since breaking up with Nate – the three or four extra evenings a week, the Sunday mornings, the nobody to call when I left work to head home – was now filled again. I had someone to touch, who liked to touch me. Admittedly it was a little less about reassuring hugs and holding hands and was perhaps, um, a little more nipple-focused than previous relationships had been. I didn't care. I felt as if I'd performed a break-up miracle.

During those two months I was very, very careful to do and say all of the right things. I always towed the party line: it's just a fling, I can stop whenever I want, I'm not going to get into another actual relationship. I repeated it to everyone who'd listen, feeling terribly racy and urbane, until I almost believed it. But in reality I didn't. Well, my brain understood the deal, but my heart was starting to get a little independent-minded and have ideas of its own. It's now perfectly obvious that in my horror at being rejected by Nate, I was just using Scott as a mirror, holding it up in order to convince myself that I still existed. Of all those late-night chats, all those lazy mornings and interminable phone calls feverishly discussing writing and films and New York City, I don't think I can actually remember what he thought about any of it. Not because I wasn't listening – I was intrigued at the time – but because all I *really* cared about was that someone was listening to me.

So, with crushing inevitability, after a couple of months I started to Get Clingy. You know what it's like, although I'm sure you'd pretend you don't. Because you always think you're being so goddamn subtle, don't you? I didn't go for the ridiculous stereotyped behaviour of the woman gripping her man's ankles, being dragged to the bar as he tries to walk up and buy a pint with his mates. It was much, much smaller than that. Oh so very subtle. It started one morning when I left the room to get my coat and leave, and I heard the flick of the kettle being turned on. Before I'd thought it through, my head had popped round the kitchen door and I was saying casually, 'Oh great – coffee! That'll stop me having to buy one on the way into work!' even though I knew it would make me twenty minutes late. What was I hoping to gain in those twenty minutes I spent awkwardly sipping coffee, sitting on the edge of his sofa? I don't know. But I couldn't stop myself doing it.

Then there was the reading of the Sunday papers. We'd have a nice Saturday night together, a nice lie-in the next morning, and perhaps we'd even go out for breakfast. At this point you are either a) his proper girlfriend, in which case you legitimately ask what he feels like doing for the rest of the day, if indeed you feel like spending it with him at all, or b) not his girlfriend so you gather your belongings and your dignity and you Just Go Home. But when you start to Get Clingy you forget that. Again, I'd think I was being really subtle when I'd suggest buying a paper, and it would seem like my plan was working, so I'd get the most heavyweight broadsheet I could possibly lay my hands on, and find myself mesmerized by every single article in it. Ta-da! An extended date! Because he couldn't possibly kick me out while I was so innocently reading, could he? It's not even as if I was talking to him

– I would just be harmlessly stroking the small of his back while I lay on the sofa. I was trying to create the atmosphere of a woman who is interested by life and all it has to offer, but only mildly bothered by him (while sneakily managing to get an extra couple of hours at his house).

Actually, I was just taking up his space when he'd rather have been reading a magazine about hi-tech electrical goods for a car he didn't own, and – imagine! – thinking about what a nice time he'd had last night. But a man can't start the actual process of missing you until you've gone. So, by forcing myself to read an unnatural amount of analysis about a bill that may at some stage have passed through the House of Lords, I was not only wasting my time and his, while not enjoying a moment of it, but I was actively nixing my chances of ever being missed.

Unfortunately, although not entirely coincidentally, this devastatingly understated new behavioural trait kicked in at just the same time as comments from him started to pop up and alert me. For example: 'I think it's so great, the way that we are both modern enough to share this time together and be so interested in each other without getting bogged down by all of that parochial stuff like commitment.' And: 'Trust me, you would *not* want to meet my parents.' I also noticed that he never seemed to have opened that copy of *Pale Fire*, despite him taking it everywhere. Was it just a prop? It slowly dawned on me that I was at the edge of a precipice and that movement in either direction wasn't looking like much fun. I could either stay and put up with more of these comments and the slow but steady drain they were putting on my confidence, or I could get out of the situation, find something to do with the vast expanses of empty time (and beds) that would open themselves up again, and sort myself out.

Up until this point I had ignored the fact that the people who'd been telling me I was so strong a couple of months ago were now starting to say things like: 'But why do you actually like him? What do you have in common?' And I'd ignored the fact that I was starting to look a bit gross – I hadn't really been eating properly since I'd broken up with Nate, I'd had a dreadful cold and I was trying to wear weird cool clothes that didn't suit – or fit – me . . . It was the same old story. I was starting to mould myself to fit into his life, instead of asking what I wanted *my* life to be like and wondering if I might like to let him mould himself into it. Honestly, why was I wearing cord trousers two sizes too big all of a sudden? The fact that they fell off my hips didn't make me look a-little-bit-street-yet-a-little-bit-ravaged-and-skinny. It made me look like a confused skater boy in a pair of trousers two sizes too big. With boobs. And what was with the faux diamanté part of that outfit? Like I said, it was a confused and spineless time for me. Undeterred, I even had an ill-advised fringe cut into my long hair. This last manoeuvre backfired on me spectacularly when Scott saw it for the first time, visibly winced as if he'd just stubbed his toe and mumbled, 'Ooooh, you're going to be fiddling with hair clips for months while you try and grow that little baby out.'

Every girl knows that the Break-up Haircut is an essential part of any healthy split. But it seems that lots of girls, including myself, don't know that the Break-up Haircut need not be the Ill-Advised Really Short And Unflattering Haircut. The talents needed to be a truly great scissorsmith are not to do with the scissors, but to do with tact and communication. This is because so many women make the misguided assumption that they need a 'new' look when they are recovering from a broken heart. This is, in most cases, wrong WRONG WRONG. When you're dumped, there is rarely a specific thing that is your fault. Just as you don't need to be radically altered internally, nor do you need to be radically altered externally either. On top of this, men on the whole prefer women to have long hair – or at least they think they do – which results in too many women equating the break-up haircut with a short haircut. Oh ladies, this can be a huge mistake: do not let it happen to you!

I speak from experience. In my time I have tried (and failed) with the following:

'The Sliding Doors'
As pioneered by Gwyneth Paltrow as Helen in the 'I've realised he was cheating' section of the movie. Of course, my version didn't work out. Because I don't look like Gwyneth Paltrow. (Apart from anything else, my neck is literally half the length.) Instead, I looked like Barbara Windsor in one of her Peggy from *EastEnders* wigs and had to grow out the cut via a kind of flapper bob. Ghastly.

'The French Kiss'
As pioneered by Meg Ryan in this and many of her other films. An unmitigated disaster for me. I quickly became easily mistaken for a crying mop.

'The Amélie'
As pioneered by Audrey Tautou as the eponymous Amélie. My then hairdresser didn't point out my huge cow's lick, so instead of having a cute, gamine cropped fringe I had an inch of hair sticking straight out of my head at a right angle. It was a terrifying interpretation of Angelina

Jolie's look in *Girl, Interrupted*, except without the added benefits of Oscars, tending to needy babies, stealing husbands, etc. Need I go on?

You get my point. Liberated, renewed and reinvented need not mean short of hair and unattractive. There are people who look fantastic with short hair, but if you haven't worked out if it suits you when you're happy and sane, you're not going to work it out when you're a gibbering mass of tears and simmering self-loathing. As any good hairdresser will tell you, what you need is someone who will chat to you and massage your scalp while they are working their magic. Above all, you need someone who will make you look the very best that you can.

If only I had known then that advice for your hair should be the same as advice for your heart: you don't need to destroy and rebuild. Just find the bits that work for you and enhance them. In other words, if you have a haircut that you actually like and that flatters you, don't get rid of it. The momentary satisfaction of seeing the hair that Nate once ran his hands through tumbling to the floor and being whisked away in a dustpan and brush didn't last. I should just have tried to be the *best* me, not a *different* me. The old one wasn't that bad.

Stung by Scott's response to fringe-gate yet unable to

face any more confrontation, I thought I'd just see him a couple more times and gently let it fizzle out. If we'd never actually been going out then there was no need for any dumping to take place, surely? But it turned out that Scott was a few steps ahead. He'd been trying the 'gently fizzling out' tactics for a good couple of weeks now, so by the time we next saw each other he'd evidently decided that I needed a firmer guiding hand out of this relationship. We were sitting in his kitchen having a cup of tea when he started talking vaguely about our 'friendship'. Then, with the subtlety of a deadly assassin dressed entirely in banana yellow he slipped in the dagger message: 'That's what we are, isn't it? We're friends. You do know that you'll never be my girlfriend, don't you?'

How could I have been such an idiot? How could I not have realized that once the decision is made you have to move fast? I'd always been amateurish at getting out of relationships but I *had* seen my dad chopping firewood – if you want to split the log properly and cleanly, one huge swing of the axe is always going to make a better cut than twenty pathetic little chops. Especially if – as I did – you want to be the one actually doing the splitting.

I was being pre-emptively dumped! How dare he actually dump me if he was so insistent that we weren't even going out? Surely it's simply not fair to dump someone who's not your girlfriend? But he had somehow managed it. And worst of all, I had nowhere to go from here. All of the conclusions I had quietly reached for myself in the dead of night were now null and void. He was calling time on the liaison.

I tried to respond with a simple: 'Yes, yes, I understand. I feel the same. I don't want you to be my boyfriend either.' Which was the truth, after all. But words fell from my mouth, echoing and hollow-sounding. The tragic irony was that now I had finally accepted the facts about our relationship, I had never sounded more like a liar. Scott looked doubtful. I didn't blame him. It seemed as if I was just agreeing with everything he said in a bizarre, sheepish endeavour to keep him. I tried repeating myself. 'No, really. I was thinking the same thing only a couple of nights ago, but it seemed a bit obvious and hurtful to mention anything. I absolutely have no interest in going out with you. I want to spend some more time alone anyway.' I'd never sounded more ridiculous. Why did everything I say sound like a lie? Why was he looking at me like that? The more I said it, the more I began to sound as if I didn't actually believe myself. But I did. My attempt at trying to reclaim the dumping, just for the sake of a little dignity, was misfiring on so many different levels. I was a brave pioneer of the Retrospective Dumping, but in reality it was never going to work. All I achieved was a dreadful case of 'the lady doth protest too much' syndrome. After about five minutes it was threatening to end in us both standing in his kitchen with our hands on our hips barking at each other.

'Fine.'

'So, FINE.'

'Well that's just FINE.'

'No no no, it's FINE.'

'Absolutely FINE by me.'

Scott practically threw me out onto the street.

Once again I was alone. Not only had I not even begun to deal with getting over Nate, but now I had the indignities of Scott to cope with too. My half-baked theories about not needing to spend time alone had proved to be nonsense – but I had been so convinced by them. How had I ever let things get so far with Scott when it had been pretty obvious all along that we weren't actually suited to each other? What's more, I had sorely tested the patience of those around me. But the trouble was, I hadn't meant to test their patience, I'd just, well, been trying to keep out of their hair, really. I didn't want to make too much of a fuss about breaking up with Nate, even though I was seven shades of gutted. So I thought I could cover it all up and get over it by simply getting a new fringe, some new trousers and swapping Nate for the anti-Nate. But now I was twice as sad. *And* I had a stupid fringe.

'How did I let it spiral out of control like this?' I pleaded of Lily when I got home that night, my hurt pride still smarting. A series of house moves and errant flatmates meant that she was currently living with me for six months, a situation that was pushing us to the outer limits of our sisterly love for each other.

'I'm not sure, but at some stage you turned into a love junkie,' she replied.

'Don't be mean! I knew we weren't in love. I suppose I was starting to feel that it would be nice if we did fall in love, but I did know that all we were doing was having sex and hanging out together.'

'Hmm, yes. But you seemed kind of dependent on it. You'd swapped one dealer for another, but your addiction was the same. You postponed the comedown, but by indulging in the high for a little longer it's now feeling all the worse. And he wasn't even all that deserving of it. It was really, really obvious that it was a rebound thing, and even though your brain seemed to get that, your heart didn't seem to understand at all.'

It was true. How could I have been broken up with Nate for so many months now, yet my head and my heart still be refusing to play nicely with each other? My head was doggedly plodding on like a very methodical child building an intricate Lego aerodrome. Meanwhile, my heart remained utterly unreliable, if not wilfully disruptive. It was behaving like the naughty, jealous toddler who keeps creeping up and kicking huge holes in the Lego aerodrome. I suppose if you were to see that child you'd be infuriated, but would think, Poor thing, it doesn't know any better. And you'd be right – sometimes your heart doesn't know any better. But there *is* a reason why. And it's science.

6

Drunk on Love:
The Science of Heartache

It's all frightfully moving for poets and romantic novelists to effuse about being 'drunk on love' and then 'going cold turkey' from a lover who has spurned you, but what actually is going on? Surely if someone can cause you to feel pain as if you've been thumped in the solar plexus, it can't merely be you being overdramatic? There must be something scientific behind it . . .

Well, ladies, the good news is that it turns out that heartache is not synonymous with being a massive drama queen. Something chemical *is* going on. It has been studied, documented and recorded. All in really boring language. So perhaps there's something to be said for those poets after all. But most importantly of all – you're not making it up! When you feel in so much pain that you might possibly die, that's because your body *is* struggling. I'm not going to lie to you, you probably won't actually die, but there's some crazy scientific shit going on when you're dumped. I for one was entirely unaware of it – or what the hell I could do to combat it – until I donned my lab coat and big geeky science goggles to investigate the science of heartache.

Just as my granny (the same one who recommended sometimes wearing no underwear) used to say – it's all down to your hormones, dear. It really is. And it's one hormone in particular: oxytocin.

Oxytocin is the Wizard of Oz of our bodies – it is responsible for dispensing the good stuff, the emotions and reactions that most of us enjoy experiencing the most. It's *specifically designed* to make you forget pain and unhappiness. But, like the good wizard himself, it also has elements that are a little bit unreliable. In fact, at times it seems like oxytocin can be downright unfair. Until relatively recently the scientific community thought that oxytocin's primary functions took place during childbirth, and that it just knocked about our systems the rest of the time. It stimulates muscle contractions, enabling labour, and is involved in the mother's production of milk. Also, crucially, it plays a huge role in the bonding process between the mother and newborn, being responsible for much of what makes us feel attached to, beloved by, or protective of other human beings.

More recently – only in the last three or four years – the boffins of the world have come to realize that actually, oxytocin plays an amazing and important role in almost all of our physiological functions. It turns out that there are two types: one is working as our antidote to stress. For example, when we are shocked or worried by something, the body produces cortisol (more of him later – he's got a bit more of a Mad Max vibe) to get us ready for action. We become alert, our breathing rate gets faster and we rapidly think through all of the best ways to deal with an upcoming drama. Basically, it's cortisol that makes you feel like you do just before a date or an exam that you are particularly keen to impress or pass. It's essential in keeping us alive or we'd get run over by buses and just roll over and die if we had a shock. However, as you can imagine, a world where we produced infinite cortisol with no brake system could become pretty scary – pretty fast. It would be like the first day of the Selfridges sale all day, every day. So after cortisol, oxytocin comes into play and calms us down. It's the hormonal equivalent of watching the *Antiques Roadshow* with a mug of warm chocolate and a crumpet after a really scary movie.

But it's the other type of oxytocin that's the *really* interesting one, because this type is specific to social interaction. It isn't just naturally released in waves throughout the day like testosterone or oestrogen are, but is dispensed according to what we are doing. So, the more we socialize with people we like – or just chat to bus conductors who seem particularly friendly – the more we produce, and so the happier we feel. It's a hippy-tastic circle of joy! (So when my mother used to come storming into my room when I was a sulky teenager, saying that I'd 'feel so much better if I got up and *did* something with the day', she was actually right. I hate to admit it, but she was. If a hormone can make you feel cheerful and loved, put a spring in your step and a smile on your face, simply by you leaving the house and chatting to someone friendly, can you imagine the mayhem it must cause if you actually hug someone? Full-on human contact, with chatting and smiling, and a nice whiff of their hormonal bouquet as well! Kerching – it's a hormonal fiesta, complete with band, crudités and a piñata.

Which leads me, predictably, to sex. The ultimate party. As far as your hormones are concerned it's a goddamn carnival. Floats, costumes and trucks filled with speakers blasting dance music. But, as ever, it's not as simple as you might think. Because when sex sends a huge whoosh of oxytocin to your party, it doesn't send it in alone. Hell, no! Why turn up solo to the best gig in town? Sex invites a whole gang of other hormones to the festivities too.

For starters, there is dopamine, which is one of the brain's reward chemicals. Dopamine is the Rocky of hormones, keeping you focused and intent on a goal. If you could see dopamine it would definitely wear sweatbands and slightly tight shorts in suspiciously flammable-looking fabric. It's dopamine that is released after physical exertion. It's dopamine whispering into your brain when you go to the gym once in a month, leading you to take a shower thinking, This is amazing! Hell, why don't I do this all the time? I'm going to start working out each morning on my way to the office. It can't be that hard to get yourself up that hour and a half earlier if you feel this great! Woo-hoo! (It is the absence of dopamine in your system that makes leaving your bed for the gym on a cold winter's day seem like such a ridiculous proposition, suitable only for Californians and trophy wives.) So, when oxytocin and dopamine come to the party in your brain together, they don't just make sex feel rewarding, but sex *with that particular person* rewarding. The one you are lying beside when these chemicals come flooding into your system becomes your focus, and your reward. And the party only gets more out of control when oxytocin and dopamine start to groove with their good-time buddies, the endorphins. These fellas are absolute party animals – they make you feel so good that they are referred to as the body's natural opiates. High praise indeed. By the time this lot have all got together in your system, you are quite the smitten kitten.

'How is this a problem? It sounds amazing, not awful? Why the hell are you telling me all of this stuff about how fantastic sex is when I've just broken up with my boyfriend and I will probably NEVER HAVE SEX AGAIN?'

Calm down, calm down – I understand your anxieties. But listen up, because here's the bit where oxytocin plays a cruel trick on us. It's absolutely, and quite literally, maddening, because as well as the aforementioned hormones being released during sex, good old-fashioned oestrogen and testosterone are also released in abundance into you and your man accordingly. BUT, in your body, oestrogen, the female hormone, prolongs and intensifies the effects of oxytocin and the way it bonds with other hormones. Meanwhile, only inches away, testosterone, the male hormone, decreases these effects significantly in your man. There is a *huge* and *infuriating* mismatch in male and female physiology:

oestrogen enhances oxytocin and all its benefits, while testosterone attacks it, meaning that a woman will tend to feel more bonded to a man after sex than a man will to her.

Effectively, it's as if you and your man are at a bar. You are drinking all kinds of crazy champagne cocktails, filled with gin and vodka and the weird blue one from the bottle at the back of the bar that no one ever orders. Meanwhile, your man is taking the advice of all the boring liver doctors who get interviewed in the papers before Christmas. He's sticking to champagne only and in between each glass he's having a pint of crystal-clear mineral water. And before he left for the bar he had a large bowl of pasta and a tablespoon of olive oil to line his stomach carefully. And he's eating a slice of wholegrain bread every hour. So, when the taxi arrives to take you home, he has a definite but gentle buzz after a night drinking classy champagne in a bar with a beautiful woman, while you are ecstatically dancing on the table with your heels dangling from one hand, a rough sketch of your wedding dress in the other and the swizzle sticks from your cocktails stuck in your hair. WHO ARE YOU CALLING IRRATIONAL?!

Exactly. It's no wonder we feel differently after sex in comparison to men. We have an entirely different set of chemical reactions going on, which, by design, affects the way in which we respond to the turn of events. We unavoidably feel the urge to focus on and attach ourselves to the man beside us, while he simply doesn't. It's not to say that men don't or can't feel bonded to women, but it doesn't become an addictive urge at such a precarious time for them. When I found myself seriously considering a relationship with Scott, and forgiving him for statements like: 'We have to run to get out of the rain; I am a singer, and must protect my voice, you know,' it wasn't because I was suddenly becoming a hugely tolerant groupie type with guacamole for brains. It was because all of our 'modern and liberated' non-committal sex had been producing chemicals designed to make me forget unhappiness and feel attached. And yet, as I learned, it wasn't having the same effect on him.

So, ladies, the rebound relationship is not simply self-indulgence, but is the action of an addict trying to find a new supplier. Your body takes a huge slump in oxytocin levels when you suddenly become single. Your constant supply of hugs, kisses and all that they lead to is cut short – usually without warning – so your ability to make all of the highly addictive and deliriously exhilarating chemical reactions that you and your body have become so accustomed to is terminated. Your body really is going through a kind of withdrawal, as potent and hard to deal with as that of any addict. And to add to the hideous cold turkey, you have an excess amount of the aforementioned cortisol in your body because of the stress. This leads to a weakened immune system, making you more susceptible to colds and stomach bugs than usual. Your sleep patterns can become chaotic and disturbed, and the quality of your skin can be affected as well.

Given that it can leave you with cravings on this scale, you won't be surprised to know that oxytocin also has a huge role to play in the ghastly phenomenon that is break-up sex. It starts with a drink to 'try and rebuild our friendship – there's so much about "us" that we don't want to lose'. But it ends with you ordering more and more drinks, just so you can stay in the bar and chat some more. Of *course* you're getting on amazingly well, there's no washing-up to be done at the end of the night and you're not nagging him to come to your uncle's fiftieth birthday with you any more. But you don't think of that at the time. You're too busy wondering if he's looking so good because he's had his hair cut, and noticing that he's wearing the shirt you gave him last year for his birthday. And remembering what it's like to be curled up in bed next to him . . . Which is exactly where you end up a few hours later. But when you roll over, overwhelmed by the feeling of forgiveness and a peaceful sense of a bond renewed, DO NOT mention Uncle Bob's fiftieth birthday party, because oxytocin is making you feel bonded to whatever is in front of you right now, and it is definitively *not* having the same effect upon him. For heaven's sake, please don't utter the words oxtyocin is bidding you to: 'I'm so glad we sorted everything out.' Because you haven't sorted everything out, you haven't even sorted *anything* out. You just had break-up sex, and he will remind you of that in no uncertain terms if you dare to suggest that it was anything else. Please don't risk it – dignity is so much more worth having.

But don't panic! Remember that for all its faults, oxytocin is not something you can only get access to via sex or boyfriends. There are tons of other ways to get it humming through your system once again.

1 Don't Forget to Leave the House

The absolutely worst thing you can do if you're nursing a broken heart is to go too far to the other extreme from a rebound – deciding against leaving the house or communicating with anyone for weeks on end. Just as it's essential to realize that rebound relationships are not real relationships, it's vital in the mending of any broken heart that you wash your hair, get out and keep seeing people who care about you and will make you laugh. Human interaction will do an enormous amount of good in keeping your old friend oxytocin from forgetting you completely.

2 *The Joy of Hugging*

If you can get a couple of bear hugs from particularly lovely male friends – or indeed warm-bosomed female ones – then you should grab them wherever possible. Cling on for at least twenty seconds for the best effect!

3 *Get Touchy-Feely*

Anything that involves a little bit of human contact will do the trick as well: dance classes, deep tissue massage, or (my personal goal) becoming one of those people who stand in pyramids on motorcycles. (Try and get to be the one in the middle – all that touching!)

4 Never Forget the Fridge

Last, but absolutely not least, there is one other way to get a little oxytocin high – eating, specifically ice cream. Yeah, yeah, you think I'm just trying to indulge you now. You think that I'm patronizing you by giving you a little treat at the end of the nerdy science chapter because you did sooo well to listen to all the complicated stuff. Well, I'm not. It's entirely true. Comfort food is called comfort food because it really does comfort. And I can even tell you why.

When your body is busy digesting something nice and easy to eat, like a gooey piece of cheese or a bowl of ice cream, your intestine secretes a digestive hormone called cholecystokinkin. It sounds like a Soviet baddy from a Bond film – particularly as scientific types refer to it as CCK, which sounds even more sinister – but I promise you that it is a hormone. When your food gets to your small intestine, the CCK sends a message to the brain via the vagus nerve. (When this was first explained to me I thought it was the 'Vegas Nerve', and cracked a ridiculous casino joke to a medical writer called Susan in San Francisco. She didn't laugh.) Anyway, the brain responds to this boost of CCK with oxytocin, blessing your body with all of the feelings of love and contentment that the hormone creates. It is worth noting that the gut has just as many oxytocin receptors as the brain does, so fatty foods are a highly efficient, if short-term solution to feeling glum. As if we hadn't worked that out for ourselves . . .

7

The Hermit Phase

My unsuccessful rebound fling and the subsequent truths it unearthed taught me that where the heart is concerned, the curve of recovery is rarely elegant. It is indeed a rather wobbly graph. There is some healthy stuff that can be achieved by a graceful little rebound relationship. But, as with the finest of heels, if you're going to experience the high, you risk an indelicate stumble.

After Scott, I really did concentrate on getting happier at being by myself. Actually, I may have concentrated a little *too* hard. In fact, I almost became a hermit.

The hermit phase is vital to any relationship recovery – mark my words, the girl who tries to avoid it only finds it creeping up on her when she least expects it, like a stealthy, clammy-handed, pubescent cousin at a family wedding. You just have to resign yourself to fate and get on with it with good grace. The trouble is that at first it's awful, but then you start to enjoy it, and it's hard to imagine ever wanting to do anything else.

Once you've accepted the fact that you've been dumped (and this can take quite a while for some) there is an inevitable period of anger often combined with frenetic partying. Your ex must only be referred to as The Fucking Wanker by absolutely anyone checking on your mental or emotional well-being, and all aspects of his personality are available for ridiculing and sneering. Elaborate fantasies about his grisly death are not uncommon. Don't be shy, use any rusty meat hook you can find – let your imagination run wild! It might sound borderline psychotic, but this phase is actually very necessary: it helps you get through the day when the pain is at its most intense. Half the time you're going home and crying yourself to sleep because the bed feels so enormous, so indulge in as much crude bitchiness with your close mates if it helps you survive.

Fun and essential though it may be, if we're honest, this stage is pretty exhausting, as I found out while trying to deal with the aftermath of both Nate and Scott together. Urgh. So it was with open arms that I embraced the hermit phase. I am quite a homebody by nature, and I wouldn't be *too* upset if I was told that I had to wear track pants and a hoodie five days a week until the end of my days. During the hermit phase you can crank that outfit up to the full seven days, baby! And it's not only that – this phase is also the time to really get to know your body hair. For a few weeks or months, you just know that you're not in the mood for getting any, so who cares what it looks like under your arms or beneath your jeans? You? HELL NO! You're finally fully single and you're starting to realize that it has its advantages. So you bin the razor. Not for ever, but for a while. The one you have probably has hairs on it that have been stroked by him, so it's best to get rid of it anyway. Whatever, I thought, I can have a fresh start later, but for now, I'm going to cultivate body hair with all the ambition of a thirteen-year-old who has designs on his geography teacher. Before long, my underarms were fit to rival those of Julia Roberts at the *Notting Hill* premiere, and if I wore tights I had hairs long enough to poke through. Indeed, if I wore jeans they practically poked through those as well.

It wasn't all about being physically grotesque, though – it was about finally realizing that I didn't have to please anyone any more. Instead of worrying about being a constant physical delight, I could relax and concentrate on things that gave me pleasure. I relished the chance to go to bed when I felt tired. When I got there, I slept diagonally, just because I could. Sunday mornings stopped being a time of sadness and emotional self-torture; they became treasured moments for indulgence: treating myself to manicures in front of old movies I'd always wanted to watch but which everyone I knew had already seen. Or taking really long-winded journeys to shops on the other side of town that sold a certain kind of cake decoration I'd always meant to buy, and spending hours on the phone to people I thought I'd entirely lost touch with. Slowly, somewhere deep inside, I was regenerating into someone who had made her peace with why things didn't work out with Nate.

I had the good luck to find a friend who was going through the hermit phase at the same time as me. Maxie was the sister of one of Nate's best friends, and when I'd starting going out with him she had just moved to London. We were the only two newcomers in their extensive and somewhat *Dawson's Creek*-esque gang of mates, so we kind of stuck to each other for company. She turned out to be one of the loveliest, funniest and most empathetic people I've ever met, so what had begun as basic survival instinct eventually became a treasured friendship. She was nursing a bruised heart at the same time as me, which meant we could have a basic level of conversation that wasn't entirely internalized and analytical. We knew we were feeling as shitty as each other, and that was what counted. We watched an awful lot of old movies together, often with a side-order of ranting and whingeing. Perhaps our choice of *Magnolia* on a rainy February Saturday afternoon wasn't ideal, but on the whole we stuck to more comforting traditional eighties fare such as *Pretty in Pink* or *Dirty Dancing*. Going through the hermit phase with someone is, I imagine, a bit like going to war with someone. You don't really want to talk about it much afterwards, but you both know what you've been through, and you respect and protect that shared knowledge no matter what.

There was one fly in the ointment. I *may* have taken the hermit phase a little too far. While I was focusing on my relationship with the sofa, replacing my addiction to oxytocin with one for *Buffy the Vampire Slayer*, my sister Lily was freshly single (having done the dumping herself – of course) and was on a delirious merry-go-round of dates and nights out with her friends, enjoying all that London had to offer. I don't regret a moment of the time I spent in The Slayer's company – she's just so kick-ass! – but the four or five episodes per night I was consuming began to get a bit excessive. Worst of all, I started to turn into my mother. Lily was my little sister, so, in the absence of anyone else to focus my affections on, I became hugely and unnecessarily protective of her. I couldn't go to sleep until I knew she was home safely. How sweet, you may think. It wasn't, because sometimes she didn't come home until 4 a.m. and she really didn't appreciate the summons from my room as she shuffled in drunk. Like the granny from '*Allo* '*Allo*, I would call her to my bedside in order to check how her night had been and if she was OK. What a joy for her. She now claims not to remember most of these chats. It's no surprise due to her passion for raspberry martinis. She was obsessed! The only trouble was that the more she drank, the more she spilt, so some nights she would look as if she'd been in a bloodbath, which was alarming, to say the least. She would try to maintain a facade of sobriety, but a quick glance at her white Birkenstocks would reveal the truth (red toes = spilt drinks), even if her slurred speech didn't. I was caring too much.

Things came to a head during an extended argument over an unwashed frying pan. Lily lost her cool and shrieked at me, 'I can't stand being monitored by you any more. You have to GET OUT THERE and leave me alone!'

Hmmm, hands moved to hips defiantly. How dare she suggest that I wasn't 'out there' enough? I had been to Maxie's only a couple of days ago for a festival of *Scrubs*-watching! I'd show her. I could still pull like the best of them. The cheek! In fact, I had been invited to a birthday party at the weekend and I would pluck the hottest man there and make him mine. I was young, had my own teeth, my own boobs, and a new pair of boots

I wanted to wear. Now I came to think of it, my friends Dave and Annie had been trying to set me up with their friend Rich for ages. 'He told Dave he wanted a nice girlfriend, just like me,' the ever-forthright Annie had whispered to me conspiratorially only a couple of weeks ago. They had introduced him to me at a party recently. I say introduced, but it was a little more erratic than that – he'd been innocently chatting to Dave, whom he'd become quite good mates with, while Annie had drunk-enly started to tug at the hem of his jacket until he paid her some attention. 'Meet my friend Alex! She's single!' she'd slurred, her eyebrows leaping up and down like a ventriloquist's doll's. Annie has a heart of solid gold but she was not blessed with the gift of tact. Rich didn't notice or didn't care, and said a brief hello to me before returning to his in-depth discussion of something gripping like Dylan going electric with Dave. So, I hadn't really got to know him, and in fact I'd been a little preoccupied by the enormous golden knot he'd made with his tie, but could remember enough to know that he was attractive and seemed nice. So, I decided, this weekend I shall have him! He's single, he has nice hair and perhaps he won't wear the tie to the party.

The mission proved alarmingly easy. Holding his gaze for just a second too long, a quick flash of my low-level knowledge of alt country music followed swiftly by a quick display of my bra strap as I fiddled with my ponytail, and a hand on his knee did it. Baby, I had it going *on*! Who knew pulling had got so easy while I'd been out of the game? Why hadn't anyone told me? By closing time we were in a cab back to my house; ten minutes after that we were in my bedroom. Seventeen minutes after that he had finished rifling through my CDs and chosen which Bob Dylan album he wanted to make out to. Thirteen minutes after that we were finished, and he was staring at my ceiling asking me if it was OK to smoke in my bedroom. Something here may as well be smokin', cos that certainly wasn't, I felt like saying. But I pushed such facetiousness to the back of my mind, determined to concentrate on the positive. Somebody wanted me!

I woke up the next morning – a little surprised to see that he'd already left – and thought, Aaaah, young love *is* what it used to be, as I tenderly remembered him telling me an unnecessarily large amount of trivia about Route 66 and the music it had inspired while we'd been in bed. I quickly moved those memories along, focusing on some other, more carnal ones. Then I wondered when he'd call so we could do it all again. I was wondering that for quite some time.

It was a couple of weeks later when I realized why I hadn't heard from the splendidly be-knotted Rich. I was having lunch with Liz, an old colleague, when I excitedly told her about my romantic exploits and of course she immediately asked who they'd been with.

'Oh, some friend of Dave and Annie's,' I casually told her, knowing that they had lots of friends in common and maybe she'd be able to enlighten me on what Rich was like.

'Oooh, tell!' was the gratifying response.

Kerching! I thought. Now I'll get the gossip . . . When I told her she looked a little startled, and then a bit sheepish.

'But he has a girlfriend!' she blurted out.

'What do you mean? Why would he do that?' I exclaimed.

'I don't know. He hardly ever talks about her. Maybe they broke up – I don't know, I don't know. I mean, I think he has a girlfriend but maybe I'm in a muddle. No, he does. And they live together. I've barely met her. I only know about her because Dominic went to university with him.' She was desperately back-pedalling, trying to shift the blame to her absent boyfriend. But I wasn't convinced.

I was upset. I started to wonder if perhaps my some-what 'direct' pulling technique (i.e. behaving about a billion times more sluttishly than I had the stamina for) had been entirely conducive to long-term commitment.

A small voice at the back of my head suggested: 'No wonder it was easy, *you* were easy . . .' How was I ever going to find out if I'd just been, quite literally, taken for a ride by him? Or if he was going to call any day soon? Or if he *had* been single and it was just a simple, if insulting, case of him just not being that into me?

It turned out that I had didn't have to wait too long to find out. A couple of months later, once my bruised pride had healed, the Frying Pan That Started The Fight had been washed up satisfactorily and I had discussed my two-timing dilemma with several friends, I saw Rich at another party I was at while still fending off a hermit phase relapse. I caught sight of him across the room and had a moment or two before he noticed me to congratulate myself. Good pull, I thought. He really was very good-looking without the ridiculous tie. Nice hair. But then, just as I started to remember the tedium of listening to his thoughts on Dylan's Never-Ending Tour, he looked up and saw me. I immediately assumed he'd be appalled to see me, even if he had broken up with his bloody girl-friend. But quite the opposite happened. He caught my eye and nodded. How curious.

A little later into the party he came up to me, kissed me hello on both cheeks and gently guided me by the elbow to a quieter area of the room. Is this guy taking the piss? I thought. Maybe he really thinks I'm incredibly stupid. What *can* he have to say?

'I was just wondering if you knew about my personal situation?' was the charming opener.

'Oh yes, yes, I found out all about the whole you-living-with-your-glamorous-girlfriend thing.'

'I hope you understand how important it is for me to protect her.'

'Excuse me? Just for reference, could I quickly check what exactly it is that you mean by "protecting" her? How does that work out for you? Is your modus operandi sleeping around? Is that what all the young men about town are calling "protecting" their girlfriends these days? I'm curious, you see.'

He gave me a little frown as if to say 'You silly, bourgeois, little girl' and explained – as if he were teaching a five-year-old about the International Monetary Fund, 'I hope you realize that it is important to me that she never finds out what went on between us.'

'I don't doubt that it is!' was all I could think of in reply.

'I hope you understand that it would be terribly indecorous of you to discuss our liaison with others.'

Now anger. Quite aside from all the nonsense that he was actually telling me, he had spoken like a gangster

rapper discussing his early years in a gospel choir, pro-
nouncing it 'In Da Chorus' instead of 'In-DECK-orous'.
Who *did* he think he was? To call me indecorous and then
say it like a freak?

'Why do you sleep around if you love her so much?
I'm not that great, and I didn't exactly mount a huge
campaign to get you, so I can only assume I'm not the
only one . . .'

Instead of replying his frown grew deeper. 'I can't
emphasize enough how important it is that you never tell
anyone we slept together.'

Did people like this *really* exist? I was beyond angry
now. I didn't care about being two-timed. I didn't even
feel embarrassed any more, as every crazy thing this man
said just made me feel better about myself by the simple
fact that I wasn't him. But I was curious – I couldn't help
delving further into his rotten mind. It was like turning
over a superficially stunning piece of exotic fruit and
finding the underside overcome with fruit flies and wrig-
gling maggots, and then not being able to tear your eyes
away.

'Well, given that you didn't take the care to even tell
me about its existence, your relationship is of absolutely
no consequence to me. While I would never do anything
to spite anyone, I'm certainly not going to *obey* you.

What happened between us is as much my personal life as it is yours.'

'I would like you to remember that I have considerably more to lose than you.'

'I would like you to remember that is something you should have thought of when you got into a taxi with me in the middle of the night.'

'Gossiping about this would be In-Da-Chorus. And inelegant.' At least he pronounced the second one correctly.

'Of course I won't maliciously gossip about you having a partner. But you must know I would never hold back any information about my own personal life from my friends if I thought that it was relevant to a conversation we were having or if it would contribute to their knowing me better. That's something you're going to have to live with.'

He sighed. 'I just don't have the vocabulary to deal with you right now.' He wandered off into the crowd.

Was what I'd said really so unreasonable that he needed a fresh vocabulary to deal with me? Of course not. The man was a lunatic. How had an argument about a frying pan led me to this parlous state of effectively being dumped again? By someone not worthy of being given the time of day, or night? I'll tell you why. It was because I was being an idiot. I had sustained the hermit phase for too long, then just blindly grabbed the first thing that came along. And I'd been grateful for it since I had no sense of my own worth. Most crucially, I seemed to have convinced myself that I deserved to get dumped.

'I have only ever been dumped once, and it was so uncool I just decided never to let it happen again,' was Lily's response to my suggestion that some girls were perhaps just born to get dumped.

Now there's the difference between Lily and me. Not only has she only been dumped once, but she was actually dumped in an incredibly funky way. She decided that it wasn't gut-wrenchingly awful, but simply 'uncool'. And she just vowed not to let it happen again, as if she was the one person with power over it.

You see, the first – and only – time Lily got dumped, everyone knew about it. She was sixteen and she'd fallen for a lad called Mark whom she thought was just about the coolest thing in the world. He was actually a posh kid from the home counties but he had pretensions to skater chic and was almost convincing us all. He and Lily became the reigning slacker king and queen at their respective schools, and Lily developed a nice line in droll *Mean Girls* humour. She never ruled the school quite as comprehensively as she might have thought, as she was too genuinely nice to have any more than a light undertone of malice, but if she'd been at high school in the US there is no doubt she would have been a power-player in the social dynamic. So, for one glorious summer Mark and Lily just hung around in their immaculately scruffed trainers and baggy jeans, adorned with colourful knotted friendship bracelets and leather-lace necklaces, talking about nothing much apart from how, like, rad, stuff was. They were totally bonded, inseparable, and really rather annoying. (I prowled in the background like a suspicious cat, wondering if Lily's love life was going to be as idyllic as this for ever.)

Unaware of the fact that a lot of the time they were stealing booze from the living room and smoking weed, my mother thought it was all rather sweet, and used one of her favourite Trinidadian expressions for them. She tipped her head to one side and proclaimed to my father that they were 'one single plait'. I smiled bleakly through a pursed mouth. They believed they were extras from *Reality Bites* who had strayed into south-east England for the summer. But they couldn't keep it up for long – for heaven's sake, the boy was a 'von' somebody! Sure enough, by the time the new term came, Mark's mother 'Miffy' (need I say more) had him packed him off to a boys' boarding school. Or at least that's what she thought. She had in fact packed him off to a boys' boarding school that had just started accepting girls.

When Lily returned to school in September she had only been there a week or so when the rumours started flying. In the end she heard from one of her least favourite classroom adversaries that Mark was planning to dump her. And of course by letting that slip, Mark had in effect actually dumped her already. Lily was crushed and mystified as to how this could have happened to her. The mystery was cleared up a couple of days later when the local newspaper ran a front-page feature about the scandal at the school.

It turned out that Mark had arrived at his posho school to find a world of opportunity away from Miffy's beady eye. Within a week he'd realized that the bounty was too plentiful to hang on for Lily during term time and had run riot among the new girls. Within the second week he'd been discovered in one of their beds by a matron with an eye much beadier than Miffy's. He was expelled and a wise-ass classmate had sold the story to the paper, knowing how enticing toff nookie would be to them.

I had left school by this stage (we went to the same one) and so I missed the fireworks that ensued, and Lily's smarting pride had been healed somewhat by the time I came home from my travels, but my mother described it as 'carnage'. Yet, with characteristic chutzpah, it only took a year for Lily to rewrite history. These days, she says, 'If you get dumped you have to be given a proper explanation because if there isn't an explanation you shouldn't have been dumped. If you receive no explanation, the way I see it, you dumped them. That gives you a chance to move on and not be hurt.'

I see what she's done there. But it's completely beyond me. There *was* an explanation for why Mark dumped her – there were loads of gorgeous girls in his class and his mother wasn't able to monitor what he was doing with them. Effectively, he'd discovered chocolate one summer and thought it was the most delicious thing he'd ever come across. When autumn came he'd realized there were different flavours, and he could pick and choose whichever one he wanted. It makes perfect sense to me. But what I believe Lily actually meant is 'if there isn't an explanation *that you like the sound of*'. I'm not saying that Lily wasn't hurt by Mark – the shredded friendship bracelets I spotted beneath her bed a year later were material evidence that she had been – but, ever an evil genius, she had somehow managed to seize all the power and control back from the situation. She believed that she didn't deserve to be dumped, so within a relatively short amount of time she'd found the vigour to turn and walk away – all the stronger.

Lily could turn heartache into a momentary blip, but I was starting to let it turn into one of my defining characteristics. I was going through every stage of a break-up and getting dumped in *all* of them. I didn't like it one bit.

8

I Will Survive:
The Healing Power of Music

Most music is about love and relationships, so of course a vast amount of those songs deal with heartache. But, when you're really in the mood to dwell, there are surprisingly few that can hit the right combination of lyrics that speak to the lovelorn and a tune that provides some kind of comfort. However, when a song does, it can change your mood in an instant. Just as every couple has 'their song' (OK, perhaps the girl thinks they do and the guy is oblivious), most break-ups have a soundtrack too. It needn't be a bad thing, it can be a heroically exciting thing!

I once entirely screwed up a job interview because an old Rod Stewart song that reminded me of an ex was playing in the background of the office. I was distraught and felt as if the song would torment me for ever. And ever. And ever. But times change. Now when I hear that song I no longer crumble into a sobbing wreck but find it quite exciting: I remember the radio, myself and the interview and think, Thank God I didn't get that job. I only went to the interview because I was so miserable. I would have been even unhappier at that company. Isn't it bizarre to think I cared so much at the time when now I feel so strong? You really do change. But it takes a while, so there are certain songs that you should *under no circumstances* attempt to listen to in public. There are some that you simply aren't ready for in the early stages of a break-up. All they will do is induce spitting rage and the throwing of perfectly innocent, possibly breakable belongings.

Here is my choice of break-up songs, complete with instructions for use.

Solitary Confinement

It is utterly forbidden for you to attempt to listen to any of the below in public. Many people don't even admit these songs exist or that they have ever heard them. Treat these people with caution – they are not cold-hearted liars, but they have nursed a broken heart and not quite come to terms with it. These are songs that act as a kind of exorcism for the very worst misery of a break-up. They are totally self-indulgent – the lyrics are utterly ridiculous. As you will now know from my opinions on the likes of Madame Butterfly and Giselle, there is simply no excuse for suicide when dumped. But let me state it again. Given some of the more dramatic proclamations of some of these songs, you may only listen to them if you swear to remember that HEARTACHE WILL NOT KILL YOU, NOR WILL YOU KILL YOURSELF. Wallow in these songs with ice cream or cheese to hand so you can administer yourself an immediate oxytocin boost as soon as the sobbing subsides. Once you have agreed to my terms and conditions, then you may listen away . . .

1 'Nothing Compares 2 U' – Sinéad O'Connor

The Mount Everest of self-indulgence. There are purists who claim to prefer the Prince original, but they're only trying to reclaim some kind of artistic credibility after admitting to liking the song at all. Sinead perfectly expresses the evil, oxytocin-induced feeling of 'No no no noo . . . it's not being loved that I need, it's being loved by YOU, and you alone . . .' If you find yourself listening to this for more than six weeks you need to think about some fresh tactics.

2 'All By Myself' – Eric Carmen

Another classic. It doesn't specifically express grief after being dumped, but does channel the feeling of anxiety after a few months of single hell when you realize that you are never, ever going to find anyone to love you and you will die cold and alone. But Eric was having you on. For heaven's sake, woman, never trust a man with hair like that.

3 'With Or Without You' – U2

Long before Bono was concerning himself with matters of state and healing world crises, he cared about much more trivial matters like being dumped. I miss that Bono. He does sound pretty gutted on this track, but I'm not sure about the continued references to how she 'gives herself away'. Is he implying that he's had the misfortune to have his heart broken by a slut? Either way, it's therapeutic melancholy listening, especially as it calls to mind the episode of *Friends* where Ross and Rachel break up. Sniff sniff.

4 'My Heart Will Go On' – Celine Dion

The only safe way to approach these lyrics is to assume that they refer to *Titanic* the movie, and that Celine's true love has in fact died, sucked under the doomed boat. Don't imagine that he dumped her; it all feels just too psychotic otherwise. Nevertheless, it provides a peerless if wholeheartedly uncool sobbing experience. Or so I've heard.

5 'If You Leave Me Now' – Chicago

We've all had days when we feel like our ex was the best thing about us. It's so easy to do when you were with a guy you really believed to be fantastic. But if he was that fantastic for you he wouldn't have wandered off and left you with nothing but memories and smeared mascara. Crank this up, wallow in the sorrow by listening to it a few times, then remind yourself that it is NOT TRUE. No one's partner is ever the best thing about them, apart from, perhaps, Kevin Federline – and even then Britney didn't escape with her dignity (or her knicker drawer) entirely intact.

6 'The Winner Takes It All' – ABBA

Oh dear God, the lyrics are almost too bitter to contemplate. No good can come from listening to this song more than once in a single day, so don't. Even then, the only real comfort that can come from this is being thankful that you are not Agnetha Fältskog, whose husband Björn Ulvaeus wrote the song, allegedly about their own marital strife, and then – when they were separated but still in the band together – presented it to her to sing. Horrid Swedish gnome man.

7 'Touch Me In The Morning' – Diana Ross

Ever had that ghastly break-up that takes place as a conversation in the middle of the night, in a bittersweet but utterly devastating way, leaving you having to stay at his house, or him at yours, until morning? Miss Ross clearly has, and she's really being brave about it, bless her. The thing is, she's not convincing anybody. This is a gorgeous song, but it's unbearably sad if you've ever been there. Once again, ladies, indulge privately or mayhem will ensue.

8 'Not Gon' Cry' – Mary J. Blige

The glory of Mary J. is that despite lots of her songs being about relationships gone wrong, almost all of them are strong, powerful anthems. This is enhanced by her fabulous bling and her inspiring self-assurance in person. (I've actually seen her perform live – the diamonds! The dress! The poise!) Sometimes I just listen to her in order to pretend to *be* her. After about fifteen minutes of nodding your head to the beat in an understanding but empowered manner anyone would feel better. 'Not Gon' Cry' is my favourite, but there's a wealth of material to choose from, for any aspiring would-be noble head-bobbers among you. If you can muster one-tenth of her dignity, composure and self-respect you will be more than fine.

9 *'And I'm Telling You (I'm Not Going)' – Jennifer Hudson*

Ladies, I cannot stress enough that this song should not be taken as advice. It is merely an expression of how you sometimes feel when spurned by someone to whom you devoted a lot of time and energy. All I'm suggesting is it might be therapeutic to listen to this and feel reassured that many others have felt the same way as you – and survived. Perhaps try cathartically singing it into a mirror, or putting the song title into www.youtube.com where you can find lots of people miming to Jennifer's version. But repeat after me: These Lyrics Are NOT Advice. You cannot simply DEMAND that somebody loves you . . .

10 'Everybody Hurts' – REM

Yeah right, like you care that everyone else has felt pain too. It's not as bad as yours, though, is it? Hmmm? You're having the worst and most painful break-up ever, aren't you? Well, maybe you are, but by now it must be time to wean yourself off this soppy phase. Maybe you should listen to this carefully, acknowledge that everybody does hurt sometimes and remember that pain is relative. Yours *will* subside, so move onto the next phase as soon as you can, OK?

Back on Your Feet

These are songs that are considerably more upbeat to listen to, and on the whole the lyrics are more positive – if a little angry. Stand up, brush your hair, and dust yourself down. It's time to dance. But beware: these songs should not be attempted *too* soon. While there is a valid and indeed essential place for anger in any break-up, it's best to make sure it is directed with caution and not at an unsuspecting DJ (unless it was the DJ who broke your heart, in which case, may I suggest 'Murder On the Dancefloor').

Although lots of these tracks are suitable for singing and dancing to, you must at all times remember that being the scary girl who won't surrender the microphone at a karaoke party until she's done 'Since U Been Gone' with a tearful rousing finale is not a good look. Nor is aggressively dancing to 'Thorn In My Side', stomping away on your own as the circle widens around you on the dance floor.

So, you should approach this selection with due prudence. Perhaps karaoke with the girls, in the car, or getting ready to go out are the best initial venues for these tracks. No need to be scared of them, though, because the day will come when you're on the dance floor with all of your mates and you suddenly hear the opening piano chords for 'I Will Survive'. And you'll realise that you *have* survived. A sweet day.

1 'Thorn In My Side' – Eurythmics

Yeah! You are finally past the Jennifer-Hudson-demanding-love phase and starting to realize that he was no good for you. In fact, he brought you down, and only served to lessen the Mighty You that was deep inside and waiting to escape. You shiver to the bone at the very thought of him

these days – no mourning here, ladies, we're
moving on. Woo-hoo, sing it loud, sing it proud!
(But don't copy that haircut. Urgh.)

2 'Tainted Love' – Soft Cell

Sometimes, it's actually you that leaves the
relationship. But that doesn't mean you haven't
been dumped – it just means you've been passive-
aggressively dumped. Someone has been so
consistently foul to you that you are left with no
option but to go. Yes, you can still love the
person, but they can also make your flesh crawl
at the very thought of the level of self-loathing
they have inspired in you. You cry for many
days, and many nights. Then you start listening
to 'Tainted Love' . . . and the clouds part. Bring it
on, Mr Almond.

3 'Yes' – McAlmont & Butler

If you were to listen to this song in the very early
days of a break-up it would do nothing more
than inspire highly toxic levels of anger: 'I will
NEVER feel better, so STOP going on about it.
You, Mr McAlmont and Mr Butler, are
participating in nothing more than malicious
taunting!' But one day you'll wake up in the

morning and realize that the heavy, tight feeling in your chest is gone. You'll open one eye, and then the other. And you still won't have thought of anything you're dreading today. You're actually looking forward to something. Yes, you do feel better. Today is the day that you listen to this song. Very, very loudly. With leaping.

4 'Since U Been Gone' – Kelly Clarkson

This is a title that could introduce a song which is either painfully tedious or outrageously exciting . . . Hurrah! It goes for the positive. Since he's been gone you've realized how wonderful your friends are, how strong you are and how much you have yet to achieve! Yeay! Kelly only really tainted the brilliance of this song by going on to release nothing but break-up songs, which makes me worry that either Simon Cowell, her manager, is really screwing with her head, or that she desperately needs some ice cream and a shag, or that her mother only listened to Alanis Morissette when she was expecting Kelly.

5 'Irreplaceable' – Beyoncé

This is about one brave man who dared to do Her Royal Beyoncé-ness wrong. The repeating of 'to the left, to the left' are not her giving him driving instructions but her determinedly dividing their possessions prior to chucking him out, and bunging all of his belongings in boxes 'to the left'. What is so fabulous is that her pain about being cheated on is every bit as tangible as her absolute conviction that he's the one who will lose out in the long run. The fact that she keeps reminding him of this is superb, and worth emulating. As is the fact that the accompanying video is unique because it's the only one where Miss B is not wearing an asymmetrical and highly flammable monstrosity designed by her mother. She always looks really cute in a pair of age-appropriate cotton trousers and a T-shirt. We *love* this Beyoncé!

6 'Train In Vain' – The Clash

Clearly about a guy who has been treated like dirt by his girl, this song could perhaps be in the boys' section of this chapter. But in the third verse, the guy starts talking about how he's got a crappy job, no nice clothes and nowhere to live. I understand the point he's trying to make, but I can't help but wonder if he was entirely blameless in this break-up. Is he just looking for

a bunk-up now? Well it won't wash with me!
Either way, it's a first-class break-up song
because it sounds like the kind of track they play
in John Hughes movies when the geeky girl is
undertaking a mighty mission in an exciting and
not at all clichéd way.

7 'Heart Of Glass' – Blondie

I merrily listened to this track for years, thinking
it was just about being a gorgeous blonde with
killer cheekbones and a breezy disdain for all silly
boys who get in the way. I suspect this is because
I was bedazzled by how cool Blondie-era Debbie
Harry is and how stunning she looks in this video.
She's one of those people whom all girls seem to
want to be. When I realized what melancholy
lyrics this track has – compared to its jaunty tune –
I loved it even more. If you can be blinded by love
and realize your heart's made of glass but remain
this spectacular then there's hope for all of us.

8 'Tracks Of My Tears' – Smokey Robinson

It might not be about a feisty and empowered
woman, but its singalong-friendly nature makes
this track a joy. The lyrics describe everything you
hope to happen when you bump into an ex at a

party: he might look like he's having the time of his life with his hot new girlfriend, but he's still hurting and yearning for you. It's not a healthy way to approach recovery, but there is always a place for fantasy from time to time, and at only three minutes long how much harm can it do?

9 'Love It When You Call' – The Feeling

I'm not ashamed to say that this song confuses me. The lyrics so perfectly encapsulate the moment when you realize that someone you thought you were all set up for a great relationship with just suddenly starts ignoring you. What did I do wrong? You were so into me? How can you just change like that with no notice? But the tune makes me leap around, filled with the excitement of a new relationship and the potential that it brings. So I concentrate on the latter, as it just about overcomes the former. I'm all for leaping, as you may have worked out by now.

10 'I Will Survive' – Gloria Gaynor

It's a soap opera in a song. It's an anthem for the lovelorn. And it scares straight boys across the land into a state of rigid terror. Nothing wrong with that – after all, hair straighteners and

tampons do the same, and where would we be
without them? So, if you don't enjoy dancing to
this once in a while then you need to take a good
look at your soul and check that it's still there.
But handle with care – abuse of this song can
lead to greater unhappiness.

When Boys Get the Blues

Clearly this isn't a list of songs that is exclusively
listened to by boys, but it's a collection of the songs
most often mentioned by boys when I queried them
('them' being friends, friends' boyfriends and total
strangers on www.myspace.com) on what had eased
their pain during times of heartache. It's an eclectic
bunch, with some surprising choices. I guess they're not
as cold as we imagine when we're lying on the floor
sobbing into the mix-tapes they once made us.

1 'Dry Your Eyes' – The Streets
This song seems to express something that boys
otherwise don't feel able to articulate at the time
that they are actually feeling it. So we should all
thank Mike Skinner for saying it out loud. It's
good for boys to have an outlet for their anguish

that isn't Grand Theft Auto or endless reruns of *Monty Python*. It's very good for girls to know that boys have those moments of anguish at all. Plus, Mike Skinner looks very cute in the video.

2 'The Needle and The Damage Done' – Neil Young

A staggering number of boys have told me this is a great break-up song. Which is odd, because I really don't know that many smack addicts. So someone's getting a wire crossed somewhere. Either a) I am unintentionally hanging out with boys who are keeping their heroin addiction cunningly hidden from me, b) I have somehow misinterpreted this song as being about heroin abuse (when it CLEARLY is) or c) boys approach relationships with the same vigour as addicts do their drugs. Which is quite touching, if somewhat troubling. Unless you're Kate Moss, in which case it must make perfect sense.

3 'I Know It's Over/Heaven Knows I'm Miserable Now' – The Smiths

There was much debate among the boys I quizzed about which of these was the better break-up song. I reached my own conclusion: it's

the former. I am perfectly aware that 'I Know
It's Over' could be either about dying or about a
relationship ending, and I know all too well that
both the arrangement and lyrics are complex,
laden with lush imagery and far too sophisticated
for me to be glib about. But holy cow, it's hard
to get to the end of this song. I would do almost
anything to avoid listening to all six – SIX! –
minutes of it. As far as I'm concerned, the reason
it works as a break-up song is because getting
dumped is an absolute picnic compared to having
to sit alone listening to this little ditty from start
to finish. The idea of anyone feeling like that *at
all*, let alone while heartbroken, is almost more
than I can bear. 'Heaven Knows I'm Miserable
Now' is a goddamn jamboree in comparison.
Thus 'I Know It's Over' wins hands down.
While I don't want to deny your right to listen to
whatever you feel like when you're heartbroken,
I neverthless beg you *not* to dwell on this one.
Unless you are male and over thirty-five in which
case I just don't have the strength to stop you.

4 'Love Song' – The Cure

I am a massive fan of lovely gothy Robert Smith,
a man who permanently looks as if he was

dumped twenty minutes ago, and it's a well-documented fact that he's got many a lad through both adolescence and heartache. In this track it's worth noting that he seems to be lavishing his compliments on his beloved once it's too late – a classic male trait. It's a very beautiful sentiment, though – and a song I imagine not many men listen to in public.

5 'Blood on the Tracks' – Bob Dylan

It's safe to say that it's pretty much impossible to choose a particular track from *Blood on the Tracks*, as the whole album works as a kind of epic, show-stopping break-up marathon. Although Bob's always shrugged off enquiries on the matter, it's widely acknowledged that the album was inspired by the break-up of his marriage to Sara Lowndes Dylan. What a marriage it must have been. I'm fairly sure that none of the items on their wedding list was left unbroken by the time they parted after eleven years together. I almost felt ashamed the first time I listened to this album the whole way through; it's so intensely personal that you feel as if you're actually in the room while they have The Talk. The utterly undisguised vitriol on 'Idiot Wind' is almost embarrassing to listen to, but the regret and melancholy in 'Tangled Up In Blue' is heartbreaking. It's wonderful, and powerful, that Dylan's able to articulate so much about the many stages of heartache, but I suggest you subtly back away from the man who professes to love this album too much. It would be just as bad as getting stuck on the dance floor with the eternally dancing 'I Will Survive' girl. Oh, and one last word of warning: should you ever get an inappropriate 'show tune' version of 'Idiot Wind' stuck in your mind, don't sing it aloud in the queue for the cinema. Boys will hate you. I know this from bitter experience.

6 'Killing In The Name' – Rage Against the Machine

I was mightily entertained by the number of men who confessed to me that, rather than sitting alone in a darkened room listening to Leonard Cohen, they like to get very angry while listening to metal records when they've been dumped. Again, this is a healthier outlet for the fury of the rejected. Top of the list of angst-rock was Rage Against the Machine. I suppose it's the male equivalent of Mary J.B. marathons. Mercifully, I haven't yet had the opportunity to put it to the test, but I look forward to hearing from any girls who have.

7 'Back For Good' – Take That

What do you mean? Why is this in the boys' section? It's sooo girly. Well, it turns out that quite a few guys are actually rather attached to this track. They don't like to shout about it, but they did confess as much (when they thought no one was listening), and they defended it vigorously when I teased them. It seems that while Robbie was conquering the world and Mark, Gary, Jason and Howard were indulging in their hobbies prior to their recent triumphant comeback, this song was getting many a heartbroken lad through the dark nights. The lyrics suggest that it was the guy who made a mess of things, or at least thinks he did; after all, a 'fist of pure emotion' does seem like a particularly mannish way to describe pain so perhaps we shouldn't be that surprised. I get a lump in my throat just thinking about the poor mites.

8 'Creep' – Radiohead

A song so depressing that Radio 1 removed it from their playlist after only two airings when it was first released in 1992. It didn't go on to be a hit for another year. This is not so much about getting dumped as not getting the girl in the first place. Hell, who am I to be so pernickety, it's all about rejection, isn't it?

9 'Last Goodbye' – Jeff Buckley

Another case of boys, um, 'not quite getting it'. Yes, this is a break-up song, but gentlemen, it's clearly about the source of your pain being regret or sadness about dumping someone, rather than about actually being dumped yourself. I can't help but think that this is somewhat revealing about how guys manage to convince themselves that they are hard done by when in fact it's actually they who have ended the relationship.

10 'Black Eyed Dog' – Nick Drake

Another song of soul-crippling sadness. We can conclude that when boys grieve for lost love, they really, really go for it. I once had the temerity to suggest that break-up songs (if not *all* songs) by Nick Drake were perhaps the most all-consumingly depressing of all, and I was told that 'he just gets a bad rep because he killed

himself'. You can imagine how unamused I was
by that.

Ones With Good Stories

1 'Cry Me A River' – Justin Timberlake

AKA Britney's cheatin' heart. As rumour would
have it, the epic relationship that was Justin 'n'
Britney came to an end when Brit started to look
for her kicks elsewhere. The fool. Because
Justin's response was to suddenly abandon the
frizz-head dork look and get really, really hot,
release a critically acclaimed and mega-selling
album, and hire a Britney look-a-like for the
video accompanying the song that is clearly
about how much she hurt him. Slick, to say the
very least.

2 'Ordinary World' – Duran Duran

It is industry gossip that this was written by
Simon Le Bon as an apology to his wife,
supermodel Yasmin Le Bon, after he cheated on
her, got busted and was thus facing life without
her, i.e. a return to the 'ordinary world'. You're

not bloody kidding – the world alone would seem very ordinary indeed if you're used to having Yasmin as your wife.

3 'Without You' – Badfinger/Harry Nilson/Mariah Carey

By now you will be well aware of my opinions on suicide as a cure for heartache: it is not a long-term solution. But it's a tragic fact that this legendary break-up song/suicide threat was written by two men who did indeed end up killing themselves. It's worth noting that in each case it is generally acknowledged that it was on account of mental instability and management squabbles within the music industry, rather than love gone bad.

4 'You're So Vain' – Carly Simon

Who was it written for? Will we ever know? There are those who claim Mick Jagger, there are those who say Warren Beatty, and there are probably lots of entertainment-industry executives wafting around California still convinced it's them. Carly actually auctioned off the answer a couple of years ago to raise money for charity. The winning bid was $50,000 and the winner had to sign extensive legal paperwork to make sure that the truth never went any further.

5 'Cool' – Gwen Stefani

If I'm listening to this song I find it very difficult to decide between a) bursting into tears at the bittersweet pain of love that has died, b) running through cornfields and skipping with joy for the peace and friendship that can come after a break-up recovery or c) doing my hair like Molly Ringwald in *The Breakfast Club* and just loving the eighties synth pop vibe. The song was written by Gwen Stefani about her ex, Tony Kanal, who was also a member of her band No Doubt, and whom she dated for several years in the early nineties. 'Don't Speak', the song that made the band in 1997, is also said to be about the break-up of that relationship, and what a difference eight years makes. Now happily married to Gavin 'Yum' Rossdale from Bush, she is reflecting on how lucky she is to still have a friendship with Kanal, and gives hope to all.

Back-up Songs For If All Else Fails:

'Hey Ya!' – Outkast

'I Feel Fine' – The Beatles

'Don't Stop Me Now' – Queen

Then there are these three. They're all ludicrous (particularly 'Hey Ya!', which has some shockingly depressing lyrics) but they will all provide immediate 'dancing around the room like a maniac' therapy. Because sometimes you're so filled with anger yet there's nowhere to direct it and sometimes you're in an insanely good mood and have no one to tell. Jumping up and down to any of these three is a good emergency measure.

9

Dumping DNA

I was really starting to dwell on this always-getting-dumped malarkey when Lily pulled me up short one day. We were walking through Regent's Park on a sunny Saturday afternoon. It was about eight months since my break-up with Nate. 'Oh, for God's sake, you just love to create problems for yourself, don't you? Getting dumped needn't actually be a part of your personality,' she barked at me.

'Hhhmmm, do you know, I actually think that it is. It all began with Tom Clay, and it's dogged me ever since.'

I was dumped by my first ever boyfriend when I was thirteen. How I got to go out with him in the first place was always bit of a mystery, because he was without question the coolest and most beautiful boy in my school. His name was Tom Clay, and he looked like a mini Greek god, or so I thought at the time. He was sporty *and* clever, and he had an incredibly glamorous older sister who had left the school a couple of years earlier. When she was still there, all the girls in my year had tried to copy her effortless, athletic cool with varying degrees of success. I couldn't believe my luck when I landed the gig as Tom's girlfriend. I should clarify. 'Girlfriend' meant 'girl with whom he held hands every now and again'. It literally was that innocent. I don't think we even kissed properly, but I was completely and utterly besotted by him. When he walked towards me some kind of hazy, dreamy music started to play in my mind. It may have been the sound of angels singing, or possibly Bananarama. I felt my knees buckling beneath me and my stomach lurch. It is of no consequence to this story that these days I can remember not one single conversation that we shared. I barely remember spending any time with him at all. But I do remember the delirious joy of waking up every morning and thinking, I am Tom Clay's girlfriend – yes, me!

It's fair to say that while I was certainly besotted, I may have been more besotted by love itself than the object of my love. Nevertheless, for one long, sunny summer in the late-eighties, we were young and in love. Until the last week of term.

During that last week we seniors were all taken on school trips to celebrate the end of our exams – and on this day Tom and I were separated. The trouble was, while we were allowed to choose which trip we took, the decision had been made at the very beginning of term before our love had blossomed. So, by the end of June, Tom was off on the sporty boys' trip to Thorpe Park, which in those days was a new and gleaming wonderland of high-tech rides and testosterone-inducing excitement. I was with my nerdy, lesson-loving friends on the bus to Wookey Hole. How could I have been so short-sighted? Of course the cool kids weren't going to go to Wookey Hole! Why would any right-minded adolescent chose a long coach trip to the West Country just to visit a bunch of stupid caves (which are of course underground) and an indoor museum about a load of old pagan folk? In high summer. Why, why, oh why would you not choose to be whizzing around on roller coasters in the sunshine? Because one trip was for cool kids, and the other not. And I was not cool.

On our return to school the next day, gossip was rife about how Tom, whose beauty was obvious to those beyond the playground, had been hit on by sixteen-year-old girls in the queue for the log flume. It took me ages to find him that day. When I finally did, I was promptly dumped. I had hunted him down inside and out and when I finally spotted him cowering in a corner of the computer room I grabbed him by the arm and tried to drag him downstairs. We were still in the stairwell when he let out a huge sob, the likes of which no thirteen-year-old boy ever wants to admit to.

'I'm so sorry, I'm sorry, I'm sorry,' was all he managed to say.

'What do you meeeeeeean?' I begged.

'I can't be your boyfriend any more. I met some other girls.'

Even in my distressed state, I noticed that he'd used the plural. Was he implying that he'd been going out with me as if I were the only girl in the world? Admittedly, I was one of only a few at the school, but still ... It was like being a character in one of those post-nuclear-world books that we always had to read. Either way, he was clearly as distraught and confused by the turn of events as I was. His complete absence of tact was only softened by Tom giving me his fluorescent rubber key ring from the Thorpe Park gift shop as a form of apology. Such innocent days.

Miss McCoy, the school nurse, found me in a sobbing heap near the computer room a short while later. I was utterly distressed and not a little frightened. The experience was much like I imagine teething to feel like – an indescribable and all-consuming pain, the origins of which I had absolutely no comprehension of and no ability to deal with. What was happening to me? Was I going to die? How could an infliction with no visible wound hurt so much? What on earth was to become of me? Help me, can you? Please? *Please?* I put these and other pressing questions to Miss McCoy as she tried to calm my uncontrollably shaking shoulders and stem the relentless tide of snot and tears. She was such a lovely lady, and I can so clearly remember her gently but firmly explaining to me that I had a broken heart, that I wasn't the first and I certainly wouldn't be the last. And then she solemnly promised me that while being dumped is the most painful of all ailments, it never, ever hurts again as much as it does the first time.

Now, I'm sure she meant well – she really was a very kind lady – but this was, quite simply, a lie. Maybe she was confused? Or maybe that was the case for her and she was just passing on ill-founded wisdom under the guise of knowledge.

Either way, getting dumped has always been just as bad for me. And by the time Lily and I found ourselves walking through Regent's Park that summer, I had come to dread it with almost every fibre in my being – to the point where it was defining me and every relationship I entered into. I had thought I was doing so well to get over Nate, but the disasters of Scott and Rich, who respresented my re-entry into the dating scene, had knocked my confidence once again. I was just getting into more of a muddle than ever.

'Don't you think it's weird? I mean, we share genes but why does your dumping DNA dictate that it just doesn't seem to happen to you, whereas it always seems to happen to me?'

My attempt to explain to Lily my struggle, my destiny and my inability to not get dumped rendered her entirely unsympathetic. 'I'm just not buying it. It's like you've given up altogether. Why don't you just stop whinging for FIVE minutes and behave like you used to when you were at university?'

'What, be drunk?'

'No, be fun. You were completely random then and you never got dumped once. You wore such weird clothes and had such dreadful make-up, but for those years you were untouchable. Your coolness had the lifespan of a boy band: for three years you managed to synthesize complete adoration, then all of a sudden it was over. The magic was gone.'

Despite her characteristically blunt turn of phrase, Lily was entirely correct. For three years at university I somehow managed to convince myself that I was incredibly cool, and thereby hoodwinked everyone else. This in turn had led to a three-year period of dumping immunity, the likes of which had never been seen since.

When I left school I went to Italy to study for a month, and I had so much fun that I decided to stay there for a few months more. A holiday job in a city built on Renaissance art and beautiful men had to be better than a holiday job in the German army barracks where my dad was posted, right? So I worked in a bar and stayed for nearly six months. I didn't speak any Italian when I arrived, and I spoke barely any when I left. The phrases I learned were entirely job-specific. I could politely ask: 'Would you like a doily beneath that bowl of peanuts?' Or: 'Perhaps you'd like an umbrella as well as a straw in your cocktail?' I remained pretty hopeless at anything other than small talk. But the language had never really been the point – it was the experience that had made me heady. For the first time I was free to do whatever I wanted, whenever I wanted. More importantly, I was able to do it where nobody knew me, so I gave myself something of a reinvention.

First of all, I started to copy how the Italians were dressing. After six years shuttling between an all-girls school – where not wearing standard issue black opaque tights was a fashion statement considered the very acme of haute couture – and a military environment where everyone was either in uniform or in camouflage, I suddenly realized that there was a world of fashion out there to be experimented with. I took it upon myself to wear almost all of it at once. I would wear strange sporty clothes that I'd seen the dancers in clubs wearing (there was a pair of silver Chipie trainers I was particularly fond of – I miss them), and combine them with old-school Italian diva make-up: at least a centimetre of deep tan foundation, black eyeliner sweeping across my upper lids à la Sophia Loren and very nude, matt lipstick. And just to add that certain pizzazz of inconsistency, I'd had my hair cropped short when I finished my A levels. The intention had been an elfin *À Bout de Souffle* look, but naturally Lily had wasted no time in telling me I looked like Mark Owen in the video for 'Babe'. She was right. But I was undeterred. Several months' worth of Italian male attention had done wonders for my self-confidence and on my return home I quickly discovered that my peers thought me dazzlingly sophisticated if my answer to the question: 'So, how's your Italian?' was a shrug followed by: 'Oh, he's very well, thank you.' It never occurred to me that I wasn't the first to try this line.

So, when I arrived at university, I was already rocking a little bit of (what I perceived to be) inimitable Euro-chic. Good for her! What could be wrong with that? I hear you cry. Well, it certainly was inimitable. And I'll tell you what's wrong with that – my interpretation of peerless Euro-chic was to arrive at my halls of residence in a black Lycra catsuit with a man-sized dark denim shirt on top, knotted slightly below the waist to create the confusing silhouette of a well-filled-out eighteen-year-old girl with both massive boobs and a huge but rather floppy knob. I was also wearing clogs. I can't even remember when, why, where or how I got them – just blame it on the Italians.

The wonder of it all is that despite being dressed like this (not forgetting my 'special' hair and make-up), because I truly thought that I was the last word in sexy continental style, I managed to persuade everyone else that I *was*. I was entirely unselfconscious, and fitted in straightaway with others I thought were as cool as me. And indeed they were as cool as me, if the definition of cool was sharing my busy schedule of fancying Chris Evans, frantically pinning posters of a pre-*Matrix* Keanu Reeves (with white Bard-like shirt and mid-length hair billowing in the breeze) on my wall, earnestly discussing John Waterhouse paintings and how sad it was that Madonna's career was totally over, and – most crucially – drinking alcopops.

I started at university the same year that alcopops were invented. We discovered them long before *Newsnight* or the uptight newspapers did. We were pioneers of binge drinking, without even knowing what we were doing. And given that we seemed to consistently clad ourselves in tiny midriff-exposing T-shirts, I'm surprised that I actually graduated with my kidneys still functioning. As far as my friends and I were concerned, those cute little bottles of booze tasted sweet, were conveniently packaged so you could dance with them in your hand much more easily than an enormous floppy plastic beaker from the Student Union bar, and they were cheap – because they were all on promotion, all of the time. Retrospectively the most amusing thing about them was that, unlike these days when they are most definitely marketed towards girls, lots of boys used to drink them too. So my best mates Ruby and Gaby and I would be out in a bar, done up to the nines in our finest party wear – perhaps some highly flammable electric-blue faux-velvet trousers or maybe a cute little lime-green shift dress made entirely of suspect man-made fibres – when we'd spot some guys standing by the bar and decide to investigate further. Mariah Carey would start trilling to a dance remix of 'Fantasy', and we'd walk past like The Pink Ladies, only deigning to look over our shoulders directly at the guys once we'd passed them. And there they'd be, leaning against the bar, with bottles of Two Dogs or Hooper's Hooch, checking us out. They would look completely ridiculous holding tiny bottles like nail polish.

Despite the ludicrousness of our outfits and pulling techniques, most of us had boyfriends by the end of the first term. Gaby didn't really have a steady boyfriend, but had had a fling with someone she fancied insanely, which ended suddenly one night when she got more drunk than she was used to after eating a big bowl of spaghetti. She has very curly hair anyway, so when she was sick it was all terribly confusing, not to mention messy – she was immediately dumped. She was deeply ashamed and swore off men for life, which lasted at least two months. Meanwhile Ruby was in a deeply toxic relationship with Hugh. He was the only man I've known to wear make-up and deny it. There were times in the mid-nineties when he was wearing almost as much foundation as I was. Hugh also had a beauty spot that didn't have an entirely consistent position on his face. It was kind of errant. But none of this was a declaration in any way – he wasn't going for the Russell Brand 'I'm such a testosterone-fuelled animal that you can't ever hold me down, no matter how much eyeliner I wear' look, nor was he making any kind of transvestite or sexuality statement. He genuinely thought that none of us noticed how he was giving nature a little helping hand. While Gaby and Ruby were with their guys, I was with my boyfriend David, who was lovely, and clearly adored me. He was fun, giggly, kind and everyone loved him. Including me.

Having someone who so openly and warmly loved me was a total novelty. After a little initial hesitation about going out with him, I became swept up in the excitement of the relationship very quickly. We had a huge group of friends whom we were each equally popular with, we went out lots and we had lots of fun messing about together. It all seemed incredibly easy, and I began to feel increasingly distant from anyone who had anything other than an idyllic relationship. It felt like Ruby was always in her room waiting for a call from Hugh, or if she was out she was worrying about the last call. David and I on the other hand were always busy with something far more important, such as buying massive water pistols to drive around town attacking people who studied Geography with. Or teaching ourselves to cook scones while ironically watching *Blind Date*. Or trying to find the best possible way to describe our hangover. (David won outright the day he announced he was 'as tired as a pillow'.) And so it was all too easy to make the mistake. Intoxicated by so much adulation from a man so genuinely kind and fun, I ended up going out with him for longer than I should have done.

What began in the first term soon stretched into the holidays – David came to stay with my family, all of whom instantly adored him. I went to stay with him at his mother's house. She was a lovely lady, but I'm pretty sure she was on to me. Then again, maybe she just didn't like the amount of attention her only son was lavishing on a girl who drank so much of her gin and had such a bizarre wardrobe ... By the end of the summer term we both decided not to go to our respective parents' houses, but to stay in my student accommodation and work for the summer in order to save up and go to New York in September. Ruby and Gaby were in London for the holidays so we had the place to ourselves and set about playing house for three months. We each got a job. I was one of thirty students waitressing in a very new and almost unbearably chic restaurant chain called Café Rouge. I got the job before the building was even finished and my face is still painted above the bar in that branch. David worked in a wine shop, which was similarly staffed and which he also loved. Before long we were in a mini-adult routine of going to work, coming back for home-cooked dinners and discussing our future together. We even took things as far as me buying lots of fancy kitchen equipment and him leaving me loving notes on the kitchen table before I left for work. We bought guide books to New York, made each other surprise Waldorf salads, watched every New York movie we could lay our hands on. We went to bed dreaming of the Chrysler Building, steam billowing from the edge of the sidewalk and long walks in Central Park. As far as David was concerned, we'd be living in the Dakota building by Christmas. How could that not be the perfect way to spend the summer?

Oh, and it would indeed have been perfect if I'd actually stayed in love with him. The trouble was that the city was deserted of almost all students, so without the merry-go-round of *Hollyoaks*-style incessant socializing, and without our audience of friends who all agreed we were 'the perfect couple', the cracks began to show. One evening when I was on my way back from work, I suddenly felt that icy cold feeling in the pit of my stomach. It was as if someone had put a large pebble in the fridge for a day, then pressed it to my naked sternum. Almost as chilling as the realization that you're being dumped is the realization that you're going to have to dump. Except it wasn't as lucid as that at first – I quickly dismissed the initial creeping feeling that summer's day as tiredness. But it did strike me as curious that these days I wasn't looking forward to being home as much as going to work.

The trouble with that creeping feeling is that once you've felt it, that's it, the feeling is out there. You can keep pushing it further and further to the back of your mind. You can never commit it to paper, never let it show and never tell a soul, but you still know it's there. You can blame it on other things, attribute it to other people and you can certainly try your darndest to disguise it as something else, but the ghastly truth remains. You know the feeling's out there. Worst of all, you're often as devastated about it as you know the person you're about to dump will be. I desperately wanted to carry on being in love with David, to carry on being his sidekick and beloved ally, to carry on the double act that everyone loved. But I was just as powerless about the fact that I wasn't in love with him any more as he was. I adored him, but with every passing day the cold feeling got stronger and stronger. I suppose it wasn't ideal to be in a relationship that was effectively ten years too old for me. It's all explicable and understandable now, but back then all I knew was that no matter what I tried, I simply couldn't conjure up the feeling of being entirely in love with him. By the time the new term began and Ruby and Gaby were back in the flat, I was at breaking point. I was going to have to end the relationship. If that was the case, it was entirely my responsibility to do it with the respect, compassion and dignity that our lovely relationship deserved. But of course I didn't: I was a total bitch.

Since the girls had come back David had moved back to the flat he was renting down the road with some of his mates. During this initial fortnight of the term I was still trying to convince myself that things could work out between us if I pushed the doubts far enough to the back of my mind. I hadn't articulated any of my anxieties to David at all, so he was ostensibly unaware that anything was wrong. But he wasn't stupid, and my enraptured enthusiasm for seeing my friends again, the way I pretty much cast him aside like a used toy when he returned to his flat and the fact that I wasn't really discussing New York any more since I decided it would be 'more exciting to go in the winter' were pretty hefty clues. This resulted in some sudden and alarmingly infantile clingy behaviour on his part. Oh great, I thought, a sweaty twenty-year-old baby on your hands, just when you're trying to show your friends the Hard Candy nail polish you bought over the summer. Just what I'm in the mood for.

Painting his bedroom a disturbingly womb-like deep red colour was a pretty bold statement of intent on his part. It merely raised my eyebrows, but Gaby's eyebrows formed a worried frown when she saw the room. Ruby was struggling to hold back knowing giggles, blind as she was then to the unfairness with which Hugh was treating her, but she certainly wasn't ignorant of what I was thinking and what David's reaction meant. His constant 'popping round to see how I was', followed by just sitting silently beside me nodding and agreeing with what I said as I chatted to my mates, started to get really claustrophobic. His continued commitment to the leaving of love notes started to seem really dumb now that my friends were back. Besides, I was by now way past needing notes to know that he loved me – the incessant patting of my hair, my thighs and my arse in front of anyone who would watch was doing that job just fine. Lest the fact that WE WERE STILL TOGETHER AND EVERYTHING WAS JUST *FIIIIIINE* had escaped any remaining members of the student body, he talked in a cutesy baby voice that had seemed adorable when it had been just the two of us with the town to ourselves. Only a couple of months ago it had been indicative of how we lived in our own private Kingdom of Love, not caring what anyone might think of us. But now, in front of the girls (or any other passing unfortunates), it was seven shades of excruciating when the beaming grin I once worshipped popped up behind my shoulder to proclaim. 'Ellllllooo vere ickle muppet!' It was so obviously excluding them, just when I was so thrilled to have their company back again. After all, we had so much to catch up on: Ruby had some PVC trousers I was dying to try on and Gaby had been to New York and brought back an avalanche of hints and tips.

Of course, it was my own selfish cowardice in not ending the relationship that was causing this craziness, and it was entirely within my power to end it. But, you see, the thing was ... I didn't want to do the dumping. I was terrified that I'd do it wrong, say something cruel, cause lasting damage. And I was really reluctant to not be the nice guy any more. I'd always set a lot of store in being a 'good' person, and as far as I was concerned, being a dumper not a dumpee would make me a 'bad' person. So I procrastinated, made sneery faces behind his back and generally behaved like the spoilt, overindulged brat that I was by then, until one day I snapped.

Let's get this clear: I definitely did not mean to be a bitch. I had no malicious ambitions whatsoever. I had in fact spent a long time trying to work out the best, kindest and cleanest way to end things. But I never found an answer I liked the sound of, so I went with the age-old classic. I told him we needed to take a break.

I was having one of my increasingly frequent girls' nights in with an assortment of ladies and a selection of *My So-Called Life* videos, when David turned up at about 11 p.m. unbelievably drunk. Apparently he'd taken it upon himself to indulge in a heroic amount of tequila. It was unclear if this had been done alone or in company, but it had most certainly been the inspiration behind a late-night 'checking on my icckle muppet girlfweeeeennd' visit. He arrived, smelly, sweaty and barely coherent. He staggered around the living room, talking over the television and behaving as if he was doing his very, very best to get dumped. Then he fell into a sulk, so I made him a cup of strong coffee and took him upstairs to my room to try and talk him into going home to get some sleep.

'What's wrooooonnnnng, why isn't my fwendly ickklle muppet pleased to seeee me any maaaaaaaaaw?' he whined.

'I am pleased to see you. I'm always pleased to see. But if you keep coming round, how am I supposed to have time to start to miss you and then be pleased to see you again?' I tactfully tried to reassure him. 'Perhaps if you came round a little less often . . . or we saw a little less of each other . . . ?' I realized I was warming up to my big D moment, and I'd forgotten all of my lines. Just as my world seemed to go blurry, David's suddenly became all too coherent.

'What? WHAT? WHAT are you saying?'

'Well, you know. It's nothing to do with you, much more, um, me, really. It's just perhaps we shouldn't be living quite so much in each others' pockets.'

'Are you leaving me?'

'No, um . . . I'm not.'

'Look me in the eyes and swear to me that you will never leave me.'

You know that bit in *Vertigo* which film buffs often talk about? You see James Stewart looking down a flight of stairs and the camera moves in as the zoom moves out. And you feel terrified. I think it's called a dolly zoom. When I looked up and my guilty, unloving eyes met David's, there was a dolly zoom moment. As in *Vertigo*, it was complete with haunting strings, or perhaps some disturbing opera music. It was playing loudly (albeit only in my mind). I knew I couldn't swear never to leave him, and I knew that not doing so would be incredibly hurtful. So I just carried on staring. Then very slowly I managed to mouth the words: 'We need. To Take. A Break.'

Moments later, David darted from the room, clearly upset and looking as though he might be sick. I've never felt so guilty in my life – he wasn't a bad person, in fact he was a lovely man. I should have been more honest with him, and done it sooner. I was a coward to have waited until I had the security of my friends around me again, and to have said nothing until confronted by him. If I had my time again I would try much harder to bear in mind that his anguish was going to last much longer than my momentary social awkwardness.

Perhaps that night taught me more than my ill-fated trip to Wookey Hole ever did: not only do I hate to get dumped, but I really, really hate to dump. I never really officially dumped David. The not saying I'd never leave him was enough. We took a break, and I somewhat coldly never really got back to him about when the break was over. He just had to work it out for himself when he saw me snogging another boy. And then another.

I never dumped anyone again during my university years, nor did I get dumped. If I wanted to stop seeing someone I stopped calling them, and given that these were the days before each and every one of us had two email accounts and a mobile phone, if they came round to my house I just asked Ruby – who had by now discovered her inner Buffy, and realized that her life was a far happier one without the overly made-up Hugh – to tell them that I was asleep until they stopped coming over. This was not good behaviour, but if it's any consolation I got my comeuppance before graduation.

It was a style dilemma that proved to be my downfall. Ruby and I were invited to an 'Ambassador's Reception' party during the last week of term. How fabulous! we thought. A homage to the student-friendly Ferrero Rocher advertisements! So off we trekked to the local charity shop, where I invested in a gold lamé and black satin ruched number while Ruby went hell for leather with some only very slightly moth-eaten velvet ruffles. It all seemed a little less funny when we arrived at the party looking like a couple of scraggy extras from *Dynasty* who'd only been let out of a dusty cupboard a few short hours beforehand, only to find that everyone else had dressed up as actual ambassadors. There were boys who'd gone out and hired full military regalia, and girls in gorgeous evening dresses. And us. 'Never mind!' we muttered to each other as we trekked home, rather itchy from our highly flammable dresses. 'Tomorrow night we shall reign supreme at the Eurotrash party!' This, we thought, was a party at which we could not fail to impress. We had spent much of the previous week preparing and had decided on some splendid outfits, as close as we could get to the kind of Euro-pop muppets that regularly appeared on the late-night Channel 4 show. I'd even decided to do my hair into little knots as a tribute to Björk. But we soon realized we'd been outfoxed once again – on arrival we immediately noticed that our hostess had an altogether different interpretation of Eurotrash, as everyone was dressed as minor European royalty, complete with suede loafers, velvet hairbands and navy blue blazers. I didn't feel at all out of place in my Junior Gaultier bustier and leather miniskirt. And Ruby was absolutely fine in her silver hot pants. Damn.

10

We Need to Talk:
What He Says vs What He Means

I once met a bloke at a party who confessed to me: 'In the past I have spent months at the end of a relationship trying to work out the best way to tell a girl I'm dumping her.'

I didn't know whether to slap him or kiss him: on the one hand I was thinking, But it's those few months when you've totally tuned out of the relationship that are the most destructive to her! She can tell that you're not into it any more, she doesn't know why and she thinks it's her! Just tell her! Then she can stop making your favourite dinners and shaving her legs and agonizing with her friends over what she's done wrong instead of talking to them about more interesting stuff like music or movies or Gael García Bernal. But there was another part of me that was grateful to hear that boys don't simply say randomly cruel things when they break up with us just for the fun of it.

Actually, it turns out that most of the time they are just as stressed as us about the break-up, and the ludicrous comments they come out with are usually a mere by-product of that anxiety. As you know, this is something I've experienced myself from the dumper's perspective. It's just that quite often I – as I'm sure do you – forget it when I'm the dumpee.

The trouble with the language surrounding break-ups is that none of it actually means that much, and a lot of it means the exact opposite of what's being said. Despite this underlying truth we cling to those final few words as if they mean the absolute world. You know what I mean – the nights you spend sobbing, repeating to yourself, 'But he said that he just needed time to think. I wonder how much time that means? Do you think Thursday is too soon? Perhaps a week? Oh God, I don't know if I can actually live without him for a whooooole week.' In retrospect, you know that he didn't actually mean he just needed some time to think. He meant that he wanted time to think about someone else, or time to think about anything but trying to make his relationship work. But it takes someone with a very strong stomach to stand in front of a person they once loved and confirm with absolute certainty that they will most definitely never want any more to do with that person *ever* again. Of course, it's easy to feel that in the heat of an argument, but it's rare to think that about someone you've felt genuine love for. So of course you soften it with a couple of 'maybe's and a 'you never know what fate might bring' for good measure.

As such, here's a brief glossary of the Language of Dumped, what it means and how to use it.

We Need To Talk

This actually means 'I need to talk, you need to listen' or 'I need to complain'. It's usually used when one party has decided they want to end the relationship, while the other is obliviously careering off into the future with wild plans about holidays. 'We need to talk' serves as the noise of a needle being ripped off an old-fashioned vinyl record, stopping the plans in their tracks and making the imminent dumpee's blood freeze as they perceive how the rest of their evening is going to be spent.

It's also used by the unwilling dumpee in a passive-aggressive dumping. When you've continually been treated badly enough that you simply don't have the fight left in you any more, 'We need to talk' can often mean 'I'm giving you one last chance to see my point of view'. It rarely works, though.

It's Not You, It's Me

A lie, I'm afraid, girls. When someone says this, what they are trying to make you feel is a sense of relief that you've done nothing wrong, you are lovely and you mustn't change. Sometimes they are gallantly trying to accept full responsibility for the heartache, but mostly they are hoping that Circumstance is going to take the blame. Circumstance can seem like such a bitch. She appears to step in when you least expect it, coming between you and your boyfriend. She's like a movie villainess, all done up in pointy patent-leather shoes with a sharp, asymmetrical bob and harsh angular jewellery. She's the one who messes things up for you when he wants to go travelling at a time when your career means that you can't, when you want to have babies but he's sticking to his guns about not wanting them at all, or when you want to move in with him but he just wants to carry on living with his *Monty Python* DVDs and his Xbox.

This phrase creates a problem: by blaming either himself or Circumstance, he encourages many of us to turn our hand to dealing with these other factors. If he's saying it's all down to him, we attempt to 'cure' him of his commitment issues or to 'teach' him why it's infinitely possible that the two of you can work things out. I'm not saying that each and every one of us is a marriage-and-baby-crazed maniac, intent on home-building at the cost of everything else that's good and sane in this world. But a woman who has just been dumped, especially a woman who wasn't expecting to get dumped, is not just mourning the loss of her boyfriend, but also the loss of an awful lot of dreams. It might not be too bad never to see his mother again, never to have to be nice to his boss again and never to have to go to his annoyingly perfect friend's house for their New Year's party again – but it's hard to give up on the dreams of a for ever spent together. So, to the grief-stricken dumpee who has just been told that she's done absolutely nothing wrong, the logical solution is to try and solve whatever *is* wrong, whether this entails several months of 'helpful' suggestions or just a lot of irritable waiting around for him to 'see sense'.

Of course, Circumstance can make relationships feel difficult or impossible. But I'm the kind of die-hard romantic who believes that if someone's extra-busy, going away for work, or having a particularly hard time in life for one reason or another, this is not the moment when a healthy relationship will wither and die like a crappy basil plant, unable to cope if left on a windowsill in a heavy storm. Circumstance isn't really a bitch after all: she usually reveals a relationship's true strengths. Anyone who is destined to make you happy will prioritize you and the time they spend with you. Work or travel is rarely an excuse – these things can always be worked out somehow. If someone is going through a tough time then they will confide in you and rely on you if they truly want to be with you. I'm so sorry to be the one to break this to you, but he *would* find a solution that makes you both happy if he really, *really* wanted to be with you. The reason for the relationship ending *is* you.

But look up! Don't despair! I don't want to lose your attention to tears! This is a GOOD thing, because when Circumstance intervenes, she doesn't gruesomely end your relationship all on her own. It's the combination of you and him that ends the relationship. Please don't think I'm a lunatic, as I'm sure this is one tough idea to swallow, but believe me – I've been there. I spent about three years thinking that Nate broke up with me because I was mugged and I didn't deal with it very well. I blamed those pesky muggers (they were only about fourteen, which is why they get to be pesky rather than actually menacing. The fact that it happened in broad daylight makes it more pesky) when in fact they had nothing to do with it at all. It wasn't them who dumped me – it was Nate. And it wasn't me who wasn't dealing very well with me getting mugged – it was Nate. But Nate wasn't a vindictive person. He didn't decide to be knowingly cruel to me when I needed him most. But he didn't love me enough, and me getting mugged made me realize it. In the end it didn't bring me sadness, it brought me freedom. You don't want to stay with a man who is not going to come up trumps when you need him. So when you hear those dreaded words, 'It's not you, it's me', don't take them at face value – they mean more than that. But in a good way.

We Need to Take a Break

Again, a phrase that is used with the best of intentions, but rarely truthfully. Perhaps a more realistic thing to be saying is 'I need to take a break from you, in order to check that I do value the idea of getting it on with someone else more than staying with you', or 'I need to take a break from you, as I'm pretty sure that I don't want you to be my boy/girlfriend any more, but I'm a bit scared about being single again so I'd like to have the option to come back if it's all a bit overwhelming for me'.

I'm not a fan of 'taking a break'. It's so synthetic. Either you break up or you don't. If you've broken up, you can always get back together – it's not as if in the event of you actually breaking up and subsequently realizing you're both still madly in love with each other, you're not going to be allowed to get back together. There is no relationship overlord who will forbid this. But there SHOULD be a relationship overlord who forbids the taking of breaks. No good can come of them – a break just means a break-up with ill-advised padding.

If you are the Break Instigator, you have everything to gain. You've clearly been unhappy in the relationship and you want to dip your toe into the waters of singledom, but you still feel great warmth and affection for your current partner so you want to keep them on hold until you've sorted your head out and decided which way you'd like to turn. Well listen up, buttercup, people don't come with pause buttons, and it's not fair to try and put someone else's life on hold. You have to either set them free or try to make it work while standing up straight alongside them. Calling for a break is the coward's way out – I should know, I've tried it.

It's a tempting approach. When you've felt the icy

stone pressed against your heart and realized that you just don't love someone enough, it can be devastating. You may even convince yourself that a break is all it will take to get things back on track. It's very, very rarely true. More generally it's just unbearably mean.

If you are the One Being Taken A Break From, you will agree to almost anything to stop yourself from actually getting dumped. It's a no-brainer! Would you like to a) spend a fortnight eating cupcakes and watching the E! channel with your best mates before returning to what you are being assured will be a radically better relationship? or b) spend the rest of your life cold and alone? Of course you take the break – how could you not?

The problem is that it leaves you entirely beholden to the whims of your once beloved. You feel utterly at his disposal, to be picked up and put down as he pleases. Aside from the implications that this might have for the future health of your relationship, it's going to give your self-esteem a right old hammering. When offered a break, decline it. Without a hissy fit (no matter how much you might feel like one). Never let yourself become his plaything, waiting for decisions while you live a weird semi-life of staring blankly at your mobile, willing it to ring. You must decide what you want out of the relationship, and see if he is either prepared or able to give that to you, rather than frantically trying to bend yourself into whatever kinds of emotional shapes you believe he'd like you to be in.

You're loving the advice on how to deal with these phrases, but the ones you're really after are the ones that are going to save the relationship. Bad news, ladies. There aren't any. If you hear any of the above phrases, it's simply too late to talk yourself back into the relationship. If you're having the conversation then the decision has been made.

There you go, I told it to you straight. I was practising being upfront and honest in case I ever have to dump anyone again. The difficulty with the actual 'moment' of getting dumped is that it is usually a long time coming. If you've been in a proper relationship, rather than just a third date kind of a situation (in which case, the preferred tactic seems to be good old-fashioned silence), then your man will not simply wake up one morning and decide to dump you. He might wake up one morning and realize that he doesn't love you like he used to, that he doesn't want to be in a grown-up relationship any more, or even that that short film he's always wanted to make is really going to have to take priority over your relationship. But he won't dump you immediately as he'll want to think about what to say.

So one day you're suddenly in a conversation that you didn't know was coming and you instantly realize that it's a conversation he's been planning. It's so unfair! You've had no time to prepare, to get your best lines polished up and ready to deliver. Urgh. Infuriating.

One more piece of bad news: all the language in the world can't stop you from getting dumped, but the way you use language *can* help to get you dumped. I'm not making these things up to upset you. I've not turned into an evil friend who only imparts bad information. But you need to know these things.

How to Get Dumped

Let me reveal to you the secret of how to get dumped. I know that if you've reached this point in the book I should perhaps assume that you don't need to be told how to get dumped, but consider this some valuable information for next time. Because you can change your behaviour – all you have to do is know what you want to change and why.

'Reinforcing messages' are the things you continually

say about yourself that make those around you see you in a certain way, when in fact it's that certain way that you are trying to avoid them noticing. In other words, you are reinforcing to them ideas about yourself that you're worrying about, despite them probably not noticing them at all. Usually, if you're shy, nervous or anxious about being seen by others in a way you believe to be negative, you'll keep mentioning it – either in order to apologize for it (thus stating that you believe you're that kind of person) or in order to answer that you're not that kind of person (thus putting that train of thought into their head when it probably wasn't there at all). The classic example of this is being told 'You look lovely today' and responding with 'Thank you, that means so much as I thought I looked really gross when I left the house'. It probably hasn't occurred to the person that you look gross, but now you've mentioned it, they'll be checking you out that little bit extra in order to see just how gross you are looking.

Relationships are a classic area in which reinforcing messages come into play. For example, if you constantly refer to yourself as someone who's always had disastrous relationships in the past, you'll begin to make those around start to think – albeit subconsciously – that perhaps these bad relationships happened to you because you deserved it, or at the very least that you are the kind of person who can take it. Likewise, if you mention your ex-boyfriend around your current one a little too often – even if you are meaning to make a flattering comparison – you can start to sound as if you're still not quite over him. I absolutely do not like the kind of guy who likes to pretend his girlfriend is entirely unsullied by anyone but himself, and who flies off the handle at the mention of any past liaisons. That's just creepy. Nor do I condone the kind of girl who deliberately keeps secrets and weaves lies about her past to try and make her current self more alluring. After all, our past and our experiences make us who we are today, so of course it's only natural to want to share when you're getting close to someone. But ladies, THERE IS A LIMIT.

For example, a constant drip, drip, drip of 'You're so much kinder than my ex', 'Thank heavens I'm with you for this hideous overnight flight delay, my ex would have gone mad' or even 'Oooooh wow, I loved it when you did that, my ex never did' will seem to you like a lovely flow of compliments. You were there – you experienced the true crapness of your ex, and you know that you're happier and saner without him. But your current boyfriend usually has no way of knowing these things. All he *really* knows is that it didn't work out. He imagines your ex to have had the body of Matthew

McConaughey (perhaps minus the tiny stubby arms – have you ever noticed them?) with the mind of a brain surgeon and the heart of a saint. Constantly reminding him of your ex will only serve to paint you in his eyes as the kind of girl who always has crappy relationships. And he doesn't want to know what your ex did, so use your language wisely – if you want to give him a compliment, just give him a compliment. Don't garnish it with a lovely stash of memories about unhappy times you'd both rather not dwell on.

'Now wait up, lady!' I hear you cry. 'Have you, little Miss Know-It-All, stopped for just one minute and considered actually practising what you preach?'

Um, well, yes. There is that, isn't there? It's a bit rich for me to be telling you not to keep going on about getting dumped and dwelling on your exes when I've written a whole book about these things. But what can I say? I did it for you. I realized what I was doing after it was too late to stop. So I carried on. And if you're reading this, Mrs Future-Mother-In-Law-Whom-I-Have-Yet-To-Meet, then, um, hi! Thinking of you!

But there may well be times when you find yourself on the other end of this messy business. Bearing in mind what we've learned about the language of getting dumped, may I recommend to you these top ten tips.

Dumping with Decency

1 Don't avoid it for too long. Give it a couple of weeks to be sure of your decision, but anything over a month is too long and you enter the risky territory of Potentially Blurting It Out At Any Minute.

2 Don't lie. What you say as your excuse will be spun in your dumpee's mind over many days and nights to come. There can be no defending planting the seed of an anxiety that needn't be there at all. For example, don't say that you're finding him clingy if you've simply got your eye on someone else. His clinginess would seem charming if you weren't batting your eyelashes at Mr Pecs-a-lot in the corner.

3 Don't give as your excuse something that you knew on the first date. 'I'm not looking to get into a relationship right now' is a classic of the genre. 'Um . . . so why did you?' is a reasonable response, so be prepared. 'I like girls with wide shoulders and narrow waists but you have a wide waist and narrow shoulders' is a more whimsical example I've experienced.

4 Don't get too elaborate. You need to give them some kind of reason, but make sure it's brief. They are going to remember what you say, mull it over and possibly repeat it to their friends (and maybe even yours). So don't tie yourself in knots trying to explain something that is essentially inexcusable as far as he's concerned. No need to dwell on the details, no matter how much you are begged and coerced into discussing it. You'll only expose yourself to the possibility of saying the ridiculous or the untrue.

5 Do it in person. Texts, emails, letters, cakes with messages iced onto them, personalized blimps and Post-its are not allowed. It's just the rules.

6 Make sure you have somewhere to be after you see them. You know about the dangers of oxytocin. So don't go dumping someone in a bar, buy them a drink to say sorry, have another five, go back to his for make-up sex, wake up apologizing and do it all again a fortnight later.

7 Don't imply AT ANY STAGE that it was anything to do with his sexual performance. Just because his skills no longer get you

frisky it doesn't mean they won't work for his next lady, so don't let him think his way is the wrong way. Unless of course he indulged in anything illegal, unhygienic or accompanied by the sounds of Kenny G. In which case, consider it your civic duty.

8 Don't try to be the nice guy. You're dumping someone; you're just going to have to accept that it's a nasty thing to have to do and the one consolation your ex has is that THEY are in the right. In time they'll realize that it wasn't going to work out and they'll stop giving you dagger stares across the room whenever you see mutual friends. But for now, don't even think about trying to get out of this with a pat on the back and a lollipop.

9 Don't Bogie your shared friends. He'll need all the comfort he can get for a while, so don't turn up wherever he's trying to have some fun and score some rebound booty. Use a little discretion and hang with your girlfriends until the most toxic of his rage has abated.

10. Don't tell him you got any of these tips from me.

11

Dumped from Celebville

I believe it was the fabulous Miss Charlotte York from *Sex and the City* who declared that it's supposed to take you half the length of the relationship to get over a man. Well, she was about right. Despite the unexpected challenges of Scott and Rich dumping me along the way, I finally completed my dance of regeneration: I got over Nate. It took about a year. Yes, ladies, I had it sorted – I was fully recovered and raring to go! I was 101 per cent over him, and there was nothing I didn't know about getting dumped. I was finally the Keeper of the Secrets to Avoiding a Broken Heart. I was a fortress of strength and feistiness – in fact, I must have known absolutely everything there was to know about the heart and its afflictions. Hit me with your best shot, guys, I'm on the market again!

But there was one eventuality I hadn't prepared for: dating a celebrity. I'm sure today's eleven-year-olds are all horrifyingly well versed in celebrity mating. Weaned on a diet of gossip mags and MySpace friends, they probably all have little glittery ring-bound folders filled with flow charts accessorized by sinister cut-outs of footballers' wives, illustrating clearly how they have developed over the years from simply being a forearm at the side of a picture to having their own hair and make-up range. These days a high-profile relationship can be a viable career option. But I was a David among an army of Goliaths; if there's one thing guaranteed to suck away your confidence, it's going out with a celebrity. If there's another – guaranteed to leave you like a shrink-wrapped sachet of neuroses – it's going out with a comedian.

It all started so well. He was a childhood friend of Dave's, and we met at Annie's karaoke birthday party. You'll know by now that Annie is a forthright kinda gal, so this was the sort of karaoke party where nobody gets away without singing. I was confused enough by it being in the basement of a Chinese restaurant in Hackney, but then there was the fact that I was in quite a lot of pain because I'd had my belly button pierced that afternoon.

My hermit phase friend Maxie and I had decided that a piercing would make a good gesture to celebrate my over-Nate-ness. Others weren't quite so keen on the

idea: my flatmate Jo was just terrified that I would somehow get it caught in a door handle and she'd be responsible for taking me – and an attached door frame –
tohospital in her knackered car. Lily – who was the only
one I was really hoping to impress with the endeavour –
just poked it and giggled. (My mother is repulsed by it.
Whenever she sees me in a bikini she panics, thinking it's
some kind of tropical bug. She has tried to swat it in the
past, but has now toned her response down to low-grade
disgust.)

I was just hoping for a quiet evening – a nice pair of
low-slung jeans and a flappy top to ease the pain in my
waist, and some chats with my mates. The last thing I was
expecting was to develop a crush on a man whose Vanilla
Ice routine was quite frankly mind-blowing. I think it
was the farmery accent. I think you'll all agree that there's
nothing as romantic as a rural Vanilla Ice.

But it's cruel of me to mock. My Toni Basil was no
less shaming: while I was actually singing the words to
'Hey Mickey' I realized what the song was about. What's
more alluring than a girl working out she's singing about
anal sex while straining to read the karaoke machine?

He wasn't famous then, he was just a guy who'd had
a show on TV. He was kind, he was funny, and, most
importantly, he didn't seem to think I was a geek. Or at
least if he did, he considered it a valuable asset. Being a

geek is nothing to do with wearing sports tops with thick-rimmed glasses, since these are all things that have been adopted by fashionistas anyway. Being a geek is a state of mind, and I can be a geek. A lot of the time it flies under the radar (unless I'm with Lily, whose geek-dar is terrifingly accurate) but much of the time it blurts out when I'm least expecting it. On a date, for instance.

So when he called and asked if I'd like to go out to eat some time, I leaped at the chance. I overlooked the slightly ominous feeling that the last guy I'd been introduced to by Dave and Annie was the heinous Rich, and hopped on the tube full of excitement. The tube was not quite so full of excitement, and waited in a tunnel idly for a good twenty minutes outside the stop. Luckily for me it was mid-summer, so I was only very slightly sweaty by the time I met him, and this was only very slightly aggravating the rash I had on my legs from lying in Ravenscourt Park all afternoon on a scratchy woollen rug with Maxie and her new boyfriend, discussing the strategy for the evening. Luckily the scalding hot bath I'd unintentionally run for myself when I got back from the park had enhanced the aggravation so my legs were quite the flaming agony as I sat down to dinner.

It was a relaxing, balmy summer's night, the kind of evening you feel might never end, when you have all the time in the world to get to know each other. How terrifying. I cracked between the starter and the main course. Disarmed by the momentary pause in conversation, I suddenly blurted out, 'This is a nightmare! I have nothing to say! I'm normally the funny one!' before shutting up immediately and looking away awkwardly, my eyes shifting from side to side guiltily like an Action Man. He was very gallant about it, and offered 'Well, you're funny too' in response. Hmmm.

Gawky outbursts aside, the evening was a success. We laughed, we kissed and we started to fall in love. But the clues were there . . . As we walked from the restaurant to a nearby pub, hoping to stretch the lovely evening out as much as we could, he asked me about my sister. Aaaaha, Lily. Finally, a topic on which I was the expert. I started to tell him all about her, up to and including the comment that friend at university made about her looking like a 'digitally enhanced version' of me. Back then, I didn't know about reinforcing messages, but as he took my hand to cross the road, instinct told me that perhaps it was a comment I should have kept to myself. He confirmed it with: 'My goodness, does she have your dazzling self-confidence as well?' At the time, I felt incredibly loved. After all, sometimes all it takes to fall in love is for someone to spot the thing that you perceive to be your biggest flaw and then profess to love it. But actually it just set the tone for the remaining two years of the relationship.

Because deep down, I still believed that I was the girl who always got dumped. Well, why not? That was what all the evidence suggested. Also, things aren't as easy as they might be when you're dating a celebrity. From the moment we got together, his success and, therefore, his fame started to rise steadily. No matter how lovely he was being to me – and for most of the time he *was* lovely – there was little that could have prepared me for the sheer weirdness of his fame. We're not talking 'Oh my God, darling, the goddamn paps are in the hydrangeas again'-type fame. Just the insidious drip, drip, drip of knowing that you're not the only one who thinks he's special and treasured. I felt an unavoidable sense of competitiveness towards the thousands of nameless, faceless teenage nerds who sat in their rooms reciting his DVDs word for word, while I was having the temerity to wonder if he'd get on well with my beloved little brother Max. After all, a childhood filled with women like myself, my mother and Lily had left Max in dire need of some fresh male company at family events, and I really wanted Mr Celeb and him to become friends. They did.

Before long, the constant push and pull began. Mr Celeb would be Mr Normal when it came to taking the piss out of me in the pub with my brother and sister, and all would be well and happy. But then something weird would happen to remind me that I was sharing him with his fans. It sounds ridiculous, but I kept forgetting that other people knew who he was. As far as I was concerned, my boyfriend was my boyfriend, not anyone else's, so I worked on the assumption that I was the only one who thought he was funny and gorgeous. If I was happiest having Sunday dinner with his lovely family, or spending the weekend helping him to paint his house, then how could anyone possibly be interested in that?

You'd be surprised. Fans are scary – not because they might sleep with your boyfriend or let themselves into your house to cut all your hair off while you're asleep, but because their love is so unconditional. We'd be walking down the street chatting – I would usually be saying something unsexy like 'Yeah, I'll defrost it but what vegetables do you fancy with it?' when three twenty-somethings dressed like extras from *Skins* would rush up, wanting to touch and hug him, professing 'I fucking love you, man', 'You're a legend', 'You're just a genius'.

Who wouldn't want to have tedious conversations with Little Miss Meal-Planner interrupted by unconditional confessions of love? Nobody. But it was a realistic option for him, and one I found very hard to compete with. Yes, I *know* all of the sensible stuff about how they didn't really know the real him, I shouldn't have let it get to me, but it's easier said than done when comedy geeks pop into your private conversations like devoted but terrifying jack-in-the-boxes. You really have to have your eye on the prize to not let things like that knock your confidence; I didn't have the stamina for the long game. Fans didn't care if he left wet towels on the bathroom floor, and they didn't worry about when he was going to take a whiffy bin bag out. They just rushed up, emitted little bursts of adoration and scuttled away again. The effect on him was visible every time: he loved the instant ego boost and was prepared to admit it.

On one occasion I was actually barged off the pavement by a gang of teenage boys who wanted to shake his hand. They just didn't care that we were having a tormented discussion about the love word, which men find so difficult to say, they just saw their idol and wanted to tell him they cared. They didn't give a toss about the fact that my heart was in my throat, my eyes were bulging with anxiety and my awesome skills of Sensible Conversation were being tested to the very limit as I tried to negotiate my way to the three words I wanted to hear most. Nor were they concerned by the big gouge left in the heel of my new brown leather boots. I was shoved aside to stand in the gutter. It really is unusually difficult to maintain your sense of self-worth when strangers are prepared to physically push you out of the way. It's even harder if they've just mangled your footwear.

I didn't help myself either. I often managed to come

out of seemingly innocent everyday interactions with my otherwise constantly pristine dignity in shatters. One day I had an almost creepy conversation with my university mate Gaby. We hadn't spoken for months when I called her up for a big catch-up. By this stage she was past her nonsensical university infatuations, was married and indeed pregnant. I was dying to tell her that after the Nate saga, I was finally seeing someone else. But before I could even get to that part of the conversation, she blurted out, 'Guess who my brother saw at the weekend?' She told me. I tried to interrupt. 'He was in the video shop with his girlfriend and she was really annoying him by doing a weird voice!' she added with relish.

I took a deep breath and did some extensive dignity-mustering. 'That annoying girlfriend was *me*. And that was in fact my excellent Tony Soprano impression, of which I am quite rightly proud.' Gaby didn't sound convinced, and nor did I.

It was becoming increasingly clear that I was a truly rubbish celebrity girlfriend. If I wasn't turning up to my first film premiere in my glasses, jeans, with no make-up and somewhat grubby hair (Mr Celeb had misread the invitation and thought it was just a screening), I was being knocked off my feet by a terrifying fleet of paparazzi who were stampeding to try and get a shot of my boyfriend with his writing partner leaving an awards event. I was a liability who didn't fit in with the other comedy WAGs, who were on the whole considerably more composed than I was.

Yes, the Comedy WAGs. They most certainly exist. While the world's media has been concentrating on footballers and their wives, a hierarchy of its own has been developing much closer to home. Call them what you will: Comedy WAGs, Gag Hags or Funny Fans. They amount to the same thing and there's every bit as much of a structure as there is among the footballers. Posh Spice's Comedy WAG equivalent is Jonathan Ross's wife Jane – she has snazzy hair, her own career, billions of kids with equally funky hair and she knows all the best gossip. Ricky Gervais's partner is too nice and normal to be scandalous, and she's had her own successful career already so she is very much the Louise Redknapp of the bunch. The rest of the UK comedy scene has an assortment of disproportionately glamorous and largely mute – but otherwise very charming – women shared out between them, as well as the pick of a shocking number of very attractive fans who are happy to throw themselves at the stars without question. Unfortunately I was very much the Melanie Slade of the bunch – inexperienced, unambitious for fame by proxy and not as lavishly dressed. For example, I attended one awards ceremony in a frock I had bought with Lily on a busy Saturday afternoon on Oxford

Street. It was gorgeous and I was really proud of it, but it seemed a little cheap when I arrived at the ceremony only to see that the other WAGs were wearing proper designers – Prada, Versace and the bloody like. To make matters worse, Mr Celeb had asked me to carry some picnic-sized pork pies in my clutch bag in case he got hungry before the end of the ceremony. So I endured the indignity of sitting at a table in my high street togs next to Noel Gallagher's immaculately dressed and coiffed partner, who was beyond confused when I began furtively rustling tin foil in my purse – eyes darting wildly – only to produce a mini Melton Mowbray rather than anything illegal.

In spite of my relentless inability to do my boyfriend proud as arm candy, he was very loyal to me, and was just as relentless in his support and belief in me. I made the decision to leave my job and go freelance and his career continued on the up and up. While he increasingly spent his days taking conference calls from Hollywood and giving interviews, I spent mine at home in grotty clothes and no make-up, panicking about whether anyone would ever hire me as a writer. He was behind me 100 per cent through the career change, and whenever I felt really down, there was always one thing guaranteed to cheer me up. My favourite game: Hide the BAFTA.

There were BAFTAs to spare around the house, so I took it upon myself to make a small gesture of nonchalance towards my boyfriend's success by hiding his awards in unlikely places and waiting for him to chance upon them. Perhaps the large pasta saucepan would have a large brass face peeking out of it. Or there could be one in the laundry basket. Maybe even the shower curtain would be pulled back to reveal his old pal the BAFTA. The fun went on for months, until he stubbed his toe on one hidden beneath the bed. I might have dropped one once as well. Oops.

As things progressed we even planned our dream trip to New York – finally! After so many trips planned and then scuppered by relationships gone awry, I was going to make it to the city I had dreamed of all this time. I was beside myself with excitement – I bought a special snuggly pair of tracksuit bottoms to wear on the plane, devoured maps of the city and was starting to choose books for holiday reading. My boyfriend was organizing for us to go and see *Saturday Night Live* filmed, we would be there for Thanksgiving and I was in charge of picking the hotel I liked the best. It was, quite literally, going to be a dream come true.

All this time, I had complete faith in his faith in me. The only problem was, somewhere along the way, I forgot to carry on having faith in myself. It wasn't as conscious as that, but deep down I assumed that, as it had always happened to me, it could only be a matter of time before

I was dumped again: so I instinctively set about trying to do whatever I could to be the model girlfriend. I decided my comedy WAG capabilities were a lost cause, so I focused on domesticity, constantly cooking an array of tempting casseroles and roasts to keep him well filled and close by at all times. When he was away filming I made sure that he always had clean sheets and clothes when he came back. Admittedly, this was partly selfish as his bedroom could get pretty gross if I didn't step in from time to time – but to be behaving like his frickin' maid? How did it come to this?

For the first few months of this behaviour, I didn't realize what a doormat I was being. To be fair, he didn't really want his sheets cleaned and ironed or his clothes folding, so I had no real need to do it. It wasn't as if he was bullying me into it. But, because he didn't really want his sheets cleaned and ironed or his clothes folding, he didn't really spot that I'd done it, so he rarely said thank you. Which brought about the next phase: the sulking. I was working so hard to try and be the perfect girlfriend but he didn't seem to be noticing, so I got a bit pouty, which as every girl in the known universe knows is SO POINTLESS. Seriously, I would genuinely love to hear from anyone who has EVER achieved anything worth achieving through the Medium of The Sulk. It really is completely and utterly useless, not to mention exhausting.

TO BE FILLED IN AND RETURNED TO THE AUTHOR IN THE EVENT OF A SUCCESSFUL ATTEMPT AT ACHIEVING ANYTHING WORTH- WHILE THROUGH THE MEDIUM OF THE SULK

I, _____, am proud to announce that I genuinely achieved _____ through the medium of sulking

I can confirm with 100 per cent honesty that:

- I DEFINITELY made it clear that I was in an actual sulk, rather than simply in another room reading a book or making a phone call with the door shut for some unknown reason
- In NO way did I exhaust myself by trying to express something possibly quite complicated, and perhaps even likely to make me feel somewhat vulnerable, through sulking – a medium that is by definition almost entirely dependent on silence and a lack of communication.
- I had DEFINITELY decided upon my goals prior to embarking on the sulk, rather than diving into an argument without really thinking it through, then realizing that things weren't going my way and storming off to reconsider my now irrational position
- At NO stage did I forget that I was in the sulk and accidentally become chirpy when something I wanted to watch came on the TV a few hours later or someone called me and cheered me up, leaving me confused as to what I was sulking about in the first place.

FURTHER QUALIFYING DETAILS

- Length of sulk: ☐ Minutes ☐ Hours ☐ Days ☐ Weeks
- Number of doors slammed: ☐
- Number of loud, huffy exhaled breaths then followed by

innocent eyes looking to the ceiling as if to say 'What me? Oh no, nothing wrong with me today': ☐

- Number of times I was specifically asked what was wrong, only to reply 'Me? Nothing? Why, should there be?' or 'Nothing, I'm FINE': ☐
- Number of times I was asked my opinion on something, only to reply 'I don't care' or 'Why are you asking me?': ☐
- Number of friends and family members who told me to stop sulking and end the problem by talking about what was wrong: ☐
- Number of those friends and family members I actually listened to: ☐
- Number of his friends and family members who I immediately pretended to come out of the sulk in front of, because I like/love/respect them and didn't want them to see me behaving in what I was starting to suspect was a slightly unreasonable manner: ☐
- Number of his friends/family members I started to flirt with in order to win support and ultimately prove ever-increasingly hazy point: ☐
- Level of satisfaction that the first twenty minutes of The Sulk brought you (1–10, 10 being the highest): ☐
- Level of satisfaction that the rest of The Sulk brought you: ☐
- Level of satisfaction that the goal you achieved has brought you since the termination of The Sulk on completion of the mission: ☐
- Level of satisfaction you suspect you might have achieved by employing The Sulk for ten minutes as a Medium to Cool Down, then taking a deep breath, thinking about what you really wanted, having a little faith in yourself and then talking about what was bothering you: ☐

I long for the day I receive one of these forms. Please go to www.queenofdumped.wordpress.com and I will tell you where to send it.

The more sulky and nervous I became, the more distant my boyfriend became. The more he focused on work, the more I focused on him. I had less and less to say about myself until my identity had become almost entirely wrapped up in his. My terror of getting dumped and having to go through it all again slowly developed into all-consuming dread until, of course, it became a self-fulfilling prophecy. I was dumped once more.

We came home from a lovely summer's evening out, shortly after he'd come back from filming. Once again, I knew something was simmering. I couldn't quite put my finger on it, but I just had that non-specific sense of trepidation that you can wake up with if you've had a dreadful dream in which something horrific happens to someone you really care about. We got ready for bed as normal while the storm clouds of anxiety gathered. The minute I got into bed I inexplicably burst into tears. Well, it wasn't entirely inexplicable: I could tell that he was now so emotionally far away from me that I was in danger of never getting him back. As his world of work whisked him ever further away – geographically and emotionally – he had less and less time for me in his life, and I wasn't blind to it. I'd been trying so hard for so long to keep up with being smiley and perky and altogether incredibly Taylor Townsend that I had finally exhausted myself. It all came tumbling out: 'Things have to change' . . . 'I can't keep this up any more' . . . it was like Nate all over again. Surely, three years later, I could get the result I was after? Couldn't I negotiate my way to a radically improved relationship this time? Couldn't I?

Of course not.

After an entirely sleepless night on both our parts, dawn came. And with daybreak came our break. He gently told me that the only way for us to proceed was for us to do the dreaded – and take a break. A sinister shiver went through my body as he suggested it. At the time I was so defeated that of course I agreed to it. Two weeks off, then we'd meet up and take it from there. But I was determined not to give up yet. I would go down fighting . . . And if I was going to do that there was one person I'd need to call: Harrie.

There is no one who know more than Harrie about triumph in the face of adversity. She's a king of hybrid between Samantha Jones and the Reverend Billy Jones. Blessed with the gift of believing she is a truly fabulous creature, yet with enough humanity to expect noting quite so splendid from everyone else, she is every girl in crisis's best friend. I met her when I was doing work experience shortly after leaving university, so she's seen me through quite a lot of my emotional upheavals. She's taken them all on her shoulders, shrugged and told me she doesn't know what I'm worrying about. She's shocked by nothing but interested in everything – and everyone. She's the only friend I have who will leave me a voicemail on a Saturday morning declaring: 'Oh God, what a *nightmare*. I had one of those days yesterday where everyone wants to sleep with me.' She remains oblivious to the fact that before she enters a room it hasn't occurred to anyone in the room that they might like to sleep with her, but an impenetrable combination of a love of life and the rock-solid conviction that everyone she encounters is probably in love with her means that by the end of any given party, most people do. This trait alone would be ghastly – but her redeeming feature is that her faith in herself is second only to her faith in her friends. Ten minutes in her company is like Viagra for the confidence. She will tell you that you can do anything, and you always believe her.

So it was Harrie I called as I sat at home in my darkened bedroom, snivelling to myself and trying to get some of the sleep I'd missed out on during the fretful night.

'You have got to get a grip!' she shrieked.

'I know, but how?' I whinged.

'It doesn't matter how. But you have to realize that you're not the only one who stands to lose out if this relationship ends. You are a beautiful, intelligent and feisty woman who has dealt with every problem life has thrown at you. You don't seem to believe that you have anything to offer your man, when in fact the relationship is nothing like as one-sided as you think. He doesn't not want you – he doesn't know what to dooo with you!'

'What do you mean?'

'He's a comedy nerd! He's the one who the girls sneered at in the playground. He's somehow ended up with this super-cool chick, who he's still probably pretty intimidated by in lots of ways, and he can't understand why his behaviour isn't pleasing her.'

'I suppose so.'

'Don't keep dwelling and panicking. Now is a time for action. He doesn't want a girl who stays at home being neurotic. He fell in love with you because you are fun, and relaxed and exciting to be with. You are no longer any of those things, so you have to use these two weeks to rediscover them. And then you will be fine.'

'I can see that you're right. I will do my best.'

So the next two weeks were devoted to seeing all the key players. I had dinner with Lily and Max. They reassured me that I was the best and most wonderful older sister in the world, then largely ignored me while Lily told us a ridiculous story about how she had got involved in a road rage attack with a man with a wooden leg. This cheered me up enormously. Jo and Sally swooped in for plentiful swearing and motivational speeches. Maxie had me over for endless cups of tea, analysis and discussion of all the things we said we'd never do again if we had to break up with another person. And my mother rang me every day to make sure I knew not to wear too much brown or beige. Excessive wearing of flesh tones will surely be my downfall as far as she's concerned. But no one really seemed to believe that a break-up was actually imminent. Least of all me.

When we met two weeks later for a long walk through the parks of north-west London, I was feeling stronger and more resilient than I had imagined I could. I was once again infected with the natural deranged optimism of the potential dumpee. I was dumped by the time we'd reached the graveyard outside the local church. It turned out that what I'd believed deep down all that time was true: I *was* the girl who always gets dumped. In that short walk, he came out with absolutely every single cliché in the book but never bothered with the actual truth: he just didn't love me enough.

I was completely and utterly floored. Mr Celeb himself had once joked that my break-up with Nate sounded like an Ingmar Bergman film, and now it was happening all over again. I had truly thought that if I recovered from Nate properly, I was now immune to the horrors of future dumping pain. How wrong I was. Because the one thing I forgot was that while there's no way at all to make yourself immune from being dumped, the most efficient way to make sure that you do get dumped is to go into a relationship while trying not to. It's just a shame I had to realize that while I was sitting on someone's gravestone, with streams of snot and tears running down my face.

I looked up at him plaintively as I realized what I really cared about. 'I suppose this means we're not going to New York then?'

The answer was no. No, we were not going to New York. It was over. And so I had to go through the whole damn charade again. My sense of defeat was crushing, only compounded by my fury that I now seemed to be running some kind of inadvertent Perfect Boyfriend Training Camp. By now almost every boyfriend I'd ever had was in a happy, steady relationship, begun after breaking up with me and hearing a few home truths. It seemed insanely unfair that their new girlfriends were reaping the rewards of my hard work while I was left picking up the pieces, and now it was going to happen all over again. Mr Celeb had successfully endured my Boyfriend Camp – he was free to sail into the breeze while I was stuck with a tub of ice cream and my Mary J. Bloody Blige CD. I simply couldn't believe that even though I knew what to do to get over a man, I now had to go through it all again: the lying beneath the coffee table weeping, the crippling self-doubt, the staggering home from parties alone convinced that everyone can tell I'm a relationship leper. This time it was even worse, as all it had done was to underline all the suspicions I'd ever had. I was almost thrilled to be proved right. I AM going to be repeatedly dumped for the rest of my life! I will DEF-INITELY die alone! My parents SHOULD be ashamed of me!

This time I was worse than ever before. I knew the details: friends, ice cream, music ... But it was the bigger picture that was bothering me now. How could I break the chain? Friends were at the end of their tether, patience frayed and eighties movies worn thin with the effort of cheering me up. I had the body of Vegas Elvis, having abused the healing power of fatty foods, and no one would dance with me yet because my 'I Will Survive' was still in the psycho phase. I was willing to try anything. It was time to bring on the big guns. I turned to self-help books.

There's no shortage of self-help books. And there's no shortage of people who hate self-help books. But somehow the two rub along together, and I actually have a sneaking suspicion that from time to time the latter may even own some of the former. Perhaps one of them is you. That's you I'm looking at, Little Miss I'm-Above-Self-Help. We all know the jokes about a bedroom shelf heaving with titles about how to *Find Love, Live Love and Be Love* or *How Your Cat's Astrological Chart Can Help You*. While I laugh at those jokes too, some of those books are dire and, at worst, not just man-repellents but general people-who-are-sane-and-lovely-repellents.

Self-help books are often rather patronizing. They can also be very humourless. The ones that do try to be funny often try too hard, which can leave you feeling a bit like your wacky art teacher is trying to crack a joke with you. But their biggest sin is that they promise too much. The key to a perfect, happy life. I have no truck with this kind of malarkey, and nor should you.

However, I quickly realized that a self-help book can be good for getting a bit of clarity about a problem when thoughts and emotions are in a terrible tangle. It's just common sense, but organized in a way that's easy to digest at a time when common sense has gone out of the window. Sometimes you need someone to point out the obvious. No author can swoop down into your life and solve everything, because then you'd be left with the belief that you can't ever sort anything out by yourself. That's no better than an over-tooled-up handyman appearing at your door just as you're assembling a complicated piece of flat-pack furniture, shoving you aside and drilling it all together perfectly. What I needed was someone who could effectively stand by and suggest 'perhaps laying out all of the planks of wood first, and then reading the instructions all the way through might help?' at the moment I was about to throw it all out of the window and devote the rest of my life to weeping in despair.

So I needed to choose carefully. And I found a couple from very different ends of the spectrum that do have wisdom and fun to impart.

The first was the frankly fabulous *He's Just Not That Into You* by Greg Behrendt. The reason this book works is because it's funny, and because it completely explodes the myth that you did something wrong to cause a break-up (or indeed, the not-getting-together-at-all-but-it-still-feels-like-I've-been-dumped). Usually it's nothing that you've done at all, and there's nothing about you that should change, but he just doesn't think you're the great fit that you do – and that's enough. The fact that the book is written by a guy, and one that seems to be nice and fun and sensible, is something of a relief and makes it a massively refreshing read.

The second is a little more, um, 'schooly'. It's *Rebuilding* by Dr Bruce Fisher and Dr Robert Alberti, and is on the whole a very wonderful book, despite its leanings towards making getting over a boyfriend feel a little bit like a geography project. This was pressed into my hands by an eager aunt when I was in the initial raw phase of heartache, and I detested it. I can tell you exactly why: it was my Lindsay Lohan-esque approach to recovery. Despite the book's very first page making me promise not to read on until I'd achieved all of the goals and accomplished all of the healing talked about in each chapter, I tried to read the entire book in one night when I couldn't sleep. I was deranged with grief and insomnia and couldn't possibly think of a reason why reading something bug-eyed and sweaty at four in the morning wouldn't have the healing effect on me that reading it, carefully considering it and then putting it gently into action over the course of a few days might do. This is NOT the way to approach self-help books.

I'm not going to pretend that *Rebuilding* is a breeze from start to finish, either. When I returned to it a few weeks after my initial insomnia fest, I immediately revisited my state of extreme anger when I got to the chapter that describes how important it is to have friends who you can 'cuss' near when you are very stressed. If anything's going to fuck me off when I'm heartbroken it's someone implying that cussing is the problem, rather than being left by a fucking arsehole of a wanker who should have bloody known better.

I think I've made my point.

But despite these flaws, when read over the course of a few months, this book turned out to be a valuable friend indeed. Even if it doesn't approve of cussing, it provides some great insights into how to reconstruct an emotional landscape when the one you knew has been utterly decimated. Just spend more than two hours on it.

After my experiences with self-help I momentarily considered investigating religion as a balm to ease my ever-aching heart. I don't suppose I'll ever know whether I really thought it would work, or if I just did it as a vague attempt at rebelling against the intense atheist beliefs of my last few boyfriends.

I went to see my local priest to get some advice about what Christianity might have to offer the heartbroken. I was hoping he'd tell me that it was the answer to everything, and I could just become dead holy until I felt better, but although he was absolutely lovely and very approachable, he promised me no such thing. In fact, he carefully explained to me that being Christian does actually mean you are still human. And that human suffering is an integral part of life. I really started to go off the whole God thing. But then he explained to me that in Christianity's eyes, human suffering is part of life because it provides us with the necessary light and shade we need to actually make the happy times feel happy. Aaaah, it started to make sense.

Next, I tried to investigate the chilled-out loveliness of Buddhism. Buddhists just seem to be so, well, *OK* with suffering. A few weeks after my graveyard dumping I had to go to a wedding that I knew Mr Celeb would be at, and I asked a friend of a friend who was a Buddhist to come with me to the wedding. I felt that I really needed an empathetic ally among Mr Celeb's friends. And he was great: endlessly sympathetic, totally non-judgemental about my fragile state, and dashing with it. There was only one problem. He was so into his Buddhism that he kept whizzing off to quiet corners by himself to scribble things into a little notebook. It was, apparently, extremely important that he was mindful about how beautiful a day it was and how lucky and happy he was. To be honest, I would have preferred him to be a little more mindful of me, but hey – he was doing me a big favour and on the whole he was a star.

Without wishing to be too trite about it, Buddhism encourages you to accept that life is going to come with an enormous dollop of suffering, no matter what you do, and that it's your responsibility to try and overcome that by achieving a combination of living a wholesome life, developing a mastery over your mind and becoming very wise. Suffice to say – as with our old friend *Rebuilding* – Buddhism is rarely going to help anyone who simply decides at four in the morning that she's had enough sobbing into her pillow and wondering where on earth she went wrong, and instead wants a little fat guy sitting cross-legged to cheer her up.

Slowly, time started to mend my broken heart and I realized that religion is basically a bit like shoes. No matter which you choose, none of them is going to have the power to make you immune to pain. It's how you respond to that pain that makes the difference – whether it's with a pedicure, discovering Jesus or a hardcore yoga holiday. Even the most spectacular handbag in the world isn't going to have the ability to protect you from the anguish of getting dumped. But – after even more time, quite a lot of ice cream and a great deal of Harrie's company – the clouds started to part and I knew I didn't need to despair. It turns out that you do actually need to know what pain feels like in order to feel happy at other times. After all, if you don't feel any anguish at the inexplicable refusal of a hot guy to give you that fifth date, then how are you supposed to feel the inexplicable delirium next time, when you realize that someone fabulous has fallen in love with you? You can't stop yourself from getting dumped. All you can do is stop yourself from living your life in the shadow of the fear of getting dumped.

12

The Departure Lounge

Ladies, I am honoured to have been your hostess and queen in the Kingdom of Dumped. But, as with all good things, your visit must eventually come to an end. No one can stay here for ever. You may be ready for it now, or it may seem like a venture to be approached in the hazy future, but have faith – you will leave my kingdom. For pity's sake, I don't want you knocking around indefinitely, reclining on my sofas and enjoying the view from the Moral High Ground, sipping the free cocktails your mates buy you in the Victim Mentality Bar or curled up in duvets in the Skiving-off-Work suites. There is a constant flow of newcomers to my kingdom, so it's only natural that you will move on to make space for those in greater need. You have lives to live! I hope you have enjoyed your stay, and I'm sure you'll always remember the time you spent here; your emotional passport will for ever be stamped with the memories of your trip and of that you should be always proud and never ashamed.

Before you leave, one final word of advice. You'll move on, and you'll find another guy. But there may be a day when you have to see your ex again, and no matter how long it may be since you left the Kingdom of Dumped, that meeting may still have the power to leave you feeling thrown or awkward.

Be prepared. Act with caution and humanity. And remember that a fleeting moment of triumphant 'Ha ha!' will fade, but a little human kindness and a killer line will go much, much further.

First of all, bear in mind that – like a mouse – he will certainly be much more scared of you than you of him, should you meet again. Guilt is a powerful dis-abler, so if you're at a party and he's refusing to acknowledge you, it may be not because he's spurning you all over again but because he fears the Wrath of the Dumped. Quite rightly . . . you may still be a simmering cauldron of dumped angst, as yet unable to approach Gloria Gaynor with any semblance of dignity and pride. Don't let this trouble you. You *do* have the ability to seize control over the situation.

Say a quick hello. Don't let him think you're scared

of him. And be nice. A little charm is never a sign of weakness in the Kingdom of Dumped, and is always much more terrifying to a dumper. Besides, he probably really cares about you – no one enjoys ending a relationship, and a dumper often still feels a lot of fondness and warmth towards a dumpee. Once you've departed the kingdom, there may yet be a chance for you to become genuine friends.

But in case it looks as if things aren't going that way, you can easily end any conversations you're not enjoying with any of these killer lines, which will be all the more effective when served with a smile and a side order of warmth.

'You're right: it *was* you not me.'

'You're right: I *am* too good for you.'

Most devastating of all is the one that lets their imagination run wild: 'Yeah, everyone's right about you.'

That could mean anything. You don't need to waste your breath describing the things that may have hurt you a year ago, or justifying your reaction to any of them. He can just mull over what everyone might have said about him, and his conscience can do the rest. Simple, but effective. And it leaves you free to depart the kingdom.

So run along now. Go and enjoy yourself. Do all of the things you wanted to, because these days there's no one to stop you but yourself.

13

The Happy Ending

There was one big demon I still needed to slay: New York City. After ten years of waiting, I worked out that I was going to have to sort this one out for myself. I *had* to get there. So I asked Lily if she'd come with me on a girlie trip. To my delight she said yes. Hurrah! The Heminsley gals were going to take the Big Apple by storm! The larks we'd have! I had fabulous 'On Broadway' images of the two of us skipping up and down Fifth Avenue swinging shopping totes to a jaunty instrumental beat; taking picnics in the park, sitting decorously on a patterned rug and smiling kindly at a small bird that lands on one of our shoulders (we were of course well trained by Monty for such an eventuality); throwing back flirty glances to professional Manhattan-type men who'd had their ties blown over their shoulders by a passing Central

Park breeze; having artistically important discussions with creative types with grubby fingernails and battered guitar cases filled with poems they'd written for us as they'd watched us choosing organic coffee from little cafés in the Village. The wealth of opportunities was mind-blowing – there was nothing the Heminsley sisters couldn't achieve on this trip. I was beside myself with excitement.

Two days later, Lily called me to say she couldn't come because of work. 'But you know, you could go by yourself,' she suggested.

'What would I do all day by myself? It would be so weird. I couldn't do any of the "On Broadway" dream stuff, or any of the romantic stuff . . .'

'Just do all of the things you've always wanted to, but prove that you can do them by yourself. Go on, I dare ya.'

She had a point. Sometimes you do just have to sort things out for yourself. And so I made it my mission. Six months later I was on my way to the airport. It was my birthday: Valentine's Day. The fact that I wasn't at home fretting on this inauspicious day was triumph alone, but this year I wasn't going to have to pretend to the postman that all my birthday cards were Valentine's cards. This year I wasn't going to have to shuffle home from work on the tube, avoiding eye contact with the smug, beaming girls carrying enormous bouquets of flowers. This year I wasn't going to have to worry that the people who'd said yes to my party might pull their usual stunt of remembering at the last minute that it was Valentine's Day and not turn up. No such worries any more. I had my flights booked and my hotel reservations made. I wasn't going to wait a moment longer for someone to take me on a romantic trip to New York. I'd saved up, I'd chosen my hotel and I was heading to the Big Apple for love and adventure.

I was delirious with anticipation and pride as I boarded the plane. I can assure you with 100 per cent certainty that in no way did I allow myself to be overwhelmed by anxiety when I saw that the top billing of the in-flight entertainment was my ex-boyfriend and his show. Oh no no noo. If I've told you once I've told you a thousand times – I am simply not the kind of lady to be thrown by such minor inconveniences as being trapped in a confined space with multiple images of my ex all around me, as all of my fellow passengers laugh and smile along. Even passing air hostesses nodded their heads with knowing amusement as they caught glimpses on the screens of those they were serving. I just opened an improving novel and kept my eyes on it. At no stage did I sneak furious, panicked or resentful glances at the screen of the businessman sitting next to me. You should know by now: I am so above that kind of fallibility. There was no sulk at all!

Realistically, there's only so long that you can keep up that level of sulking when you're alone, so before long I was again genuinely giddy with excitement. Even so, nothing prepared me for the elation I felt when we landed. I was totally overwhelmed when I saw the huge Stars and Stripes hanging in the passport checking area. Friends and family had given me thorough warnings to be exceedingly respectful to the sarcastic and potentially aggressive staff at Port Authority, and I was determined to get through customs with the absolute maximum amount of my dignity in tact. So when the disarmingly smiley guard asked me how I was, I shocked myself when I blurted out a huge sob and announced to him (and indeed the people about seven deep in the queue behind me): 'I'm fine! I just can't believe I'm here! I tried for ten years but I kept getting dumped!'

As two plump tears landed on my passport I was ushered away with great haste. I felt like someone who'd turned up at Ellis Island with a maimed leg, clearly demonstrating my inability to work and improve the nation. I imagined myself in the petticoats of 1910, fresh off the boat, being eyed up by the guard as he whispers to his awesomely moustached colleagues, 'She keeps getting DUMPED. Shall we let her in?'

The fastest way through customs is not necessarily the most dignified.

I mustered strength as I headed for the taxi queue, determined to get New York City on my side. So when I reached the front of the queue and the yellow cab pulled up alongside me, I hopped in and started gabbling. I must have asked about a thousand questions, and he answered barely one. He truly was the most taciturn taxi driver of all time. I saw medals dangling from the rear-view mirror alongside his rosary. I'm pretty sure that one read 'Silent Taxi Champion 2005'.

This whole New York jaunt was really beginning to make my spirits dip. And then we emerged from the Holland tunnel. He turned round, winked at me, then slammed his hand on the horn. 'YEAH BABY!' he shrieked. 'You made it baby! You're in Manhattan now! And you're going to take New York City by storm!' Then he turned his eyes back to the road, and remained silent for the rest of the journey.

I was startled, but greatly heartened. He got it! And as I looked out of the window, I realized that even if I wasn't actually going to take New York City by storm, there was already some sort of a storm going on. Snow was pouring out of the sky.

As the taxi pulled up to the hotel I felt consumed by nerves. I was so proud that I was staying in this fancy hotel, paying for myself and entirely independent from the whims of a man. But I was also aware that it was, well, quite weird to be checking into one of the most romantic venues in New York City all by myself. The check-in process only served to compound my anxieties. The constant 'Just the one case?', 'Just you in the room?', 'Are you expecting any guests?', 'Just one for breakfast then?' began to echo in my head, getting louder and louder until I was sure that all anyone in the swanky Soho loft-style lobby could hear was the relentless repetition of 'JUST YOU? ALL BY YOURSELF? JUST YOUOOOOOOUUOUU?'

But I got over that when I saw all the lush cosmetics in the bathroom. I mean, seriously, how depressed could I have got? Did you *really* think I was going to be down for long? It was bloody gorgeous in there! The minute the super-camp concierge had left the room, I leaped on to the bed, splayed my arms and legs and took a moment to wallow in my achievements. Yeay! I was starting to be the me I'd always dreamed of being – a successful writer with the chutzpah and the means to do for myself the things I used to rely on boyfriends to sort out for me.

At this point in my delightful realization I passed out, the jetlag effortlessly getting the better of me. I woke up confused but with a sense of being utterly indestructible.

I set out into Soho, casually trying to imply – by my

gait – that I was a native New Yorker. 'Yeah yeah yeah, I know where I am, I played on these streets as a child' was what my lolloping hips were saying, but my mind was another matter. 'Oh my GOD. Check it out, that's actually Spring Street! Shit – all the taxis *are* yellow!' I was mesmerized, and wandered around Soho and Little Italy for a couple of hours, knowing that uptown was yet to be conquered. The thought of all those streets named after numbers was making me feel a bit giddy, but all of that changed as I was walking up Broadway and again turned my head left.

There it was, the Chrysler Building. Just there, at the other end of Broadway. It glinted in the glare of the sunlight and snow, and I felt sure it was winking at me. It knew that it was the image on my ironing board cover. It knew that when I broke up with my last boyfriend and Sally had encouraged me to take the photograph of him out of the beautiful art deco frame he'd given me for my birthday, I'd replaced it with a doodle of me at the building. It knew I had made it, and I had done so regardless of the knocks I took along the way. All those times I was being dumped and my emotions felt like a snagged jumper caught in a car door, unstoppably unravelling before me, suddenly seemed worth it. Because each and every one of them had given me the get-up and go to give myself this moment. I was so thrilled to have made the city mine: it's never going to be the city that so-and-so showed me, or the place I refer to at parties as the one I went to with an old boyfriend once. It's my city. Then I saw a taxi coming and leaned back into the pavement. Oops.

After my Moment of Chrysler Triumph I headed uptown for a further challenge. I was itching with excitement to go to Tiffany's. I wanted to prove to myself that I would wander around that temple to romance and – for Lily's sake and for mine – not feel sad that I was there alone.

One thing's for sure: you're never alone in Tiffany's, as the place is crawling with tourists. Undefeated, I wanted to wallow and look at every single floor. So, after an initial panicked meander around the ground floor, frustratedly peeking between the sturdy jackets of monolithic Midwesterners, I headed for the lift. A handful of tourists and a couple joined me. The liftman asked me what floor I was going to and I asked for the top of the building. Next he asked the couple. Simultaneously the guy said 'third' as the girl said 'fourth'. The doorman, whom I now realize had been carefully primed for this moment, looked at them and said, 'But the fourth floor is christening gifts, and the third is engagement rings.'

The girl looked puzzled, but realized what was happening when she saw her boyfriend get on his knee before her in the crowded lift. The guy took her hand and looked up at her. 'I know,' was all he said.

She realized she was being proposed to and burst into tears, the guy hugged the liftman and all of the tourists started to clap and cheer. It was a lot to fit into a journey between two floors, but I like to think we worked as a team and made it one of the most special days of that girl's life.

As I was walking back to my hotel, I stopped into a shop to buy some make-up that Lily had asked me to get for her. The shop was on a corner and the frontage was almost entirely glass. As I entered, I saw a man on a ladder thoroughly cleaning the two clear glass walls, his ladder somewhat perilously wedged into the snow which had been heaped up off the road and onto the pavement. I was very careful not to knock him off. As I was paying for Lily's goods, there was an enormous clatter as he fell off from quite a height. Everyone in the store spun round in horror – was he OK? There was a ghastly pause. I thought of Steve Martin falling off his Cowboy Dan horse towards the end of *Parenthood*. And then he leaped up! Just like Steve Martin, the window-cleaning man was fine. We all breathed a sigh of relief and gave him a burst of applause, then I strolled back to the hotel.

Should I have been saddened that I was in the city I'd wanted to visit with every love of my life, and it was strangers around me who were receiving proposals?

Maybe. Should I have been sad that I was buying cosmetics for Lily instead of sharing a funny moment like that with her? Maybe. But I wasn't. I just felt as if the city was showing off for me. It seemed eager to dazzle me with just how many dreams it could make come true, keen to earn the faith I had always shown in it.

Until what happened next. When I got back to my room I kicked off my shoes, threw my coats onto the plush oatmeal-coloured sofa, and went to look through the bits and pieces I'd bought that day – some coffee for Max, moisturiser for my mother, an I ♥ NY T-shirt for Harrie and so on. Then I reached for my wallet to take the receipts out – and realized it wasn't there. How on earth could I be managing to have the blood-running-cold feeling on this trip that meant so much? How could New York do this to me? I had clearly had my wallet snatched. I felt like Travis Bickle in *Taxi Driver*, nothing but bile and anger welling up inside of me as I realized I'd been stung. I tipped all of my bags upside down, desperately hunting through everything, unable to see clearly through the mist of tears now appearing. Gutted gutted gutted.

I called my bank and cancelled my cards, silently despising the little gits who were running riot with my cash and my dreams through the Big Bloody Apple. Then, with horror, I recognized that I'd have no way to pay my swanky hotel bill. I felt more alone than ever before. How on earth was I going to get out of this predicament? Clearly, I was totally incapable of travelling alone and looking after myself like the independent woman of class I'd kidded myself into thinking I was. All hopes of happiness or dignity now cast asunder, I fled downstairs to the front desk, barefoot and crying. I explained my predicament to the girls there, and they were overwhelmingly lovely to me. Within seconds they had asked me where I'd last used the wallet, called the store and been told I'd left it at the till when the window-cleaning man had fallen off his ladder. So charmed was I by the day I was having, I had forgotten the simple practicalities of life. Whoever said I was a dreamer?

I got my wallet back, and the third round of applause of the day was a delicate, discreet and somewhat classy one from the front-desk staff at the hotel. I wasn't alone in New York. People had helped me out and the city hadn't scorned me like I'd thought. Nor was I entirely incompetent. OK, so I may as well have lost my wallet, given that all my cards were now obsolete, but the hotel showed astonishing humanity and simply told me I could pay when I got back home. They didn't make me feel like an idiot. In fact, they made me feel like a hero, as it was yet another challenge I'd proved I could face alone. I *was* becoming the me I'd always wanted to be. If a little slowly.

On my last morning I went on a specific mission that I'd set myself for the trip. I wanted to walk through Central Park in order to go and stare at the Dakota building and chuckle to myself about how ten years ago David and I had dreamed of living there one day. (Seriously, were we on crack? Or were we planning careers as ace international diamond smugglers? Because I can't imagine what else would have given us the impression that we had a hope in hell of living there . . .) I realized I was pretty hungry from the cold, and stopped to buy a pretzel. As I sludged back from the pretzel stand and headed back in towards the park, I wondered again if I should be feeling sad that I wasn't holding hands with the man of my dreams. Should I be feeling like more of a failure that it had been ten years of break-ups that led me here, rather than a man with a mission to dazzle me? Perhaps not, I decided. I reckoned I was doing OK on my own.

Just as I was thinking this, I heard a man's voice behind me.

'Excuse me, ma'am, are you going to the ice rink?'

Ooooh, this is it, I thought! I could be about to meet the man of my dreams – right now! In Central Park! I'm being picked up. We'll go ice skating together but I'll be crap at it so I'll fall into his arms and then we'll have our first kiss! Oh, it will be the most wonderful story to tell our children and grandchildren as we all walk through the park together every Christmas Eve.

'Um, no. I'm heading west actually. But I . . .' I turned around and realized that it was not in fact the man of my dreams, but a rather portly park official, carrying some litter on a stick.

'Ooooh, your accent – where are you from, ma'am?'

'London. I'm from London.'

'I LOVE London!'

'Me too! It's my home.'

'THE EASTENDERS! I love it because of the *EastEnders*!'

I frowned, puzzled by his sudden enthusiasm for cockneys.

'I watch it on BBC America! I love Sonia!'

With that, he was off. Leaving me in the snow and the trees, holding a pretzel. And then it suddenly dawned on me how excited I'd been in that split second when I realized that I had the whole of the best relationship of my life in front of me. I have no idea who it will be with. But I know that one day soon, I'll have that feeling again – the inexplicable fizzy feeling that bubbles up inside you when you're falling in love. It's as if you've eaten popping candy, but it's affecting your whole body. I understand that this is also perhaps an accurate description of someone experiencing the bends – but you know the feeling I mean. It's when you lean in, hoping he is leaning in too – not knowing but prepared to take the risk. Then your lips touch, and a tiny voice at the back of your head is saying, 'Oooooh, I wonder if this is my last first kiss?'

You haven't failed at romance until you've given up trying. As the trees parted and I stared up through the snow at the Dakota building, I knew that of course I haven't failed, because I'm far from giving up. Love isn't rational – that's kind of the point. If you could just summon it up when it's convenient, then where would the fun be? I realized that I want – indeed, I love – the inconvenience. I want the struggle, because it's there that the romance lies. Anyone can book a first-class flight to New York for their girlfriend, just to keep them quiet, but just imagine how great my next boyfriend is going to be now that I got to New York City all by myself.

In that moment I felt more proud of myself than if I had been able to buy one of those Dakota apartments – because of three things. I knew I would never let the fear of getting dumped rule my life any more, I knew that I had got this far without being bitter, and, best of all, I had the pride and excitement of knowing that I haven't yet had my last first kiss.

Acknowledgements

The greatest, warmest thanks must go to my family for their immeasurable love and support. To my father, for your endless reserves of patience and your confidence in me when mine failed; to my mother, for your lifetime of love, guidance and drama – you are not a demented windmill but a suave goddess; to my sister, for the shameless insights, fleeting adoration and fun times thrust upon me – if you weren't my sister I could only dream of having you as a friend; to my brother, for your good-natured tenderness over a lifetime of flouncing women, your company in some of my darkest hours, and your grace when you realized I had spent longer on the canary than you in this book – you are beyond tanders.

There are several others I'd like to thank: Ivan Mulcahy for grasping my idea so early on and finding the right balance of threats and hilarity to get me writing it down; Ingrid Connell for her infectious enthusiasm and

ACKNOWLEDGEMENTS

support as I relived some ghastly experiences; and Dusty Miller, Ellen Wood and the team at Macmillan for laughing at me in the right way.

The experts who gave the benefits of their enormous wisdom: Helen Perkes, Susan Kuchinskas, Christianne Ganteaume, Father Phelim Rowland and Lee Stafford. And Priscilla and Angela at the Mercer.

The girls who provided such invaluable kindness and encouragement during what I now like to refer to as my 'Extensive Research Years': Melissa Weatherill, Georgina Moore, Sophie Deveson, Vanessa Langford and Caroline Grist, as well as early cheerleaders Sarah Ballard, Clare Bennett, Mirren Delaney, Joanna Ellis, Katy Follain, Alice Fisher, Natalie Ganteaume, Nikita Lalwani, Zoe Ornstein, Georgie Palmer, Lesley Thorne and Polly Vernon. The tears mopped, drafts read and advice given never went unappreciated even if I seemed busy having tantrums.

The boys who have done valiant work soothing my occasional bouts of 'They're All The Bloody Same'-itis: Laurence Creamer, Max Deveson, John O'Connell, Michael Grist, Fergus Gilroy, Oliver Lambert, Nigel Stoneman and Matt Thorne. Your determination that I Can Do Better and your enthusiasm for this project never failed to raise my spirits.

And the Mr Right I will one day meet: thank you for overlooking the fact I committed all my exes to paper.

Visit **www.panmacmillan.com** to read more about all our books and to buy them. You will also find features, author interviews and news of any author events, and you can sign up for e-newsletters so that you're always first to hear about our new releases.